The Sweetest Hangover

By

Monique Lawton

ISBN: 1-4033-4823-5 (e-book)
ISBN: 1-4033-4824-3 (Paperback)

Library of Congress Control Number: 2002092874

This book is printed on acid free paper.

Printed in the United States of America
Bloomington, IN

1stBooks – rev. 10/28/02

This book is dedicated to the man that emerged from a sea of chaos and made calm the waters of my life. Thank you Walter, I am complete.

Acknowledgements

To my family and friends who have supported me and thought that I was brilliant, Walter Jr., Walter III, Wesley, Tawann, Cynthia, Mommy and Daddy, Cecil, Catina, Valerie, Natasha, Lawrence Stoner, Gary and Ruby Manning, and Tyler.

Warmest thanks to 1st Books for presenting this opportunity and helping in fulfilling my dreams. Thanks Kevin for fixing my computer to help meet my deadline. To all of the people in my life, past and present who have contributed to my warped imagination and perception of life, thanks and no thanks. This is the first of many to come, watch out because here I come. Thank the Lord.

Table of Contents

I.	I Must Be Slipping	1
II.	Me, Myself, and I	9
III.	I'm Fine The Way I Am	16
IV.	The Meeting	21
V.	A Celebration	28
VI.	Hello My Darling	32
VII.	Time	37
VIII.	Pinch Me	42
IX.	How Slow Is Slow?	47
X.	Good Friends	51
XI.	It's On	58
XII.	It's Morning	64
XIII.	Nothing like 'Em	68
XIV.	Slumber Party?	73
XV.	Life Is So Good	79

XVI. Not What It Seems.............................. 84

XVII. When? 89

XVIII. Back? 94

XIX. Sad Songs 98

XX. Goodbye Yesterday 104

XXI. You, Me, and He... 108

XXII. Reunion.. 114

XXIII. A New Day.. 117

XXIV. Here We Go Again 123

I Must Be Slipping

"Oh no", I thought to myself as I sat at the bar and watched this skinny, Michael Jordan wanna be, with a football shaped head walk up beside me. "I am not in the mood for this bullshit." I mumbled to myself. I hoped he would notice that I was not interested, but so much for wishful thinking because he continued to walk up to me. "Is this seat taken baby?" He said leaning in around the bar stool so that his face was in mine, "You looked like you needed some company, so I decided to waltz on over and introduce myself. I'm Stan, you know as in *the man.*" He extended his hand toward me smiling with a crowded mouth of teeth and gums as if what he said was supposed to be charming. "Look Stan, or is it *The Man?* I have not had a very good day. I know that I am sitting at this bar alone, and that may seem like I want somebody to come on to me, but I really came here to clear my head and be *alone.*" I waived my hand as to say, "you're dismissed", but he did not move and sat his butt down. "Easy baby girl. I was just trying to brighten your day. You need to get off that high horse and give a brother a break." What did he say that for? I swung the stool around and stood up waiving my finger. "I was trying to be nice, but let me break it down for you *Brother.*" I said in my most ghetto sounding voice. "I just told you that I wanted to be alone. What is your malfunction in life that you don't understand, LEAVE ME ALONE? I'm so tired of

1

you lame ass scrubs with your lame ass come on lines. Get the hint. Better yet, you don't have to leave because I'm gone. There's your break, *Brother!*" I snatched my purse up and stormed toward the coat checkroom. As I walked off I could hear him say, "Damn, some fool got you all fucked up!" And of course he was right. As I left the bar I couldn't help but to think about what had happened between Fabian and myself these last couple of days. Fabian was the type of guy who always knew what to say. He made everybody feel like they were the most important being on this earth when he talked to them. I guess that's why I fell so hard for him. He was my type of guy, light-skinned with the most pitiful looking brown eyes and a smile that would knock you back with those pretty pearly whites. His words would pour out of his mouth like sugar. I don't think I ever heard him speak a bad word about anybody. His arms and hands were the parts of him that I enjoyed the most. I always felt so safe and warm in them, like that was the only place I wanted to be. Any time that we had a falling out about something, he knew he could just hold me and I would submit to him. But Fabian had his faults. He was just too into pleasing everybody else, especially other women. I don't think he was ever pleased with himself. Deep down, I knew what type of man Fabian was. But he knew how to pacify me and he knew exactly what to say and do to make me forget anything he may have done wrong. I always knew that something was being hidden from me. Something Fabian had been through made him react to people the way he did. I didn't believe that he loved people the way he put on, but I could never put my finger on it. And Fabian damn sure wasn't volunteering any information. So I just let it go because hey, if he didn't want to talk about it and he was fine with it, so was I. But, you can only be a fool for so long before you get a wake up call. All of his secrecy started causing problems. Problems that led to many nights with me sleeping alone and Fabian coming home in the late hours with all kinds of idiotic excuses.

I don't know if I was just naïve, scared of losing him, or just plain stupid. All the signs were there telling me that he was sneaking around. He would leave his job around 6:00 and call me around 8:30 telling me some stupid story about him meeting his friends for drinks or he was helping a friend fix his car. Fabian was too fine to be under somebody's hood and he knew it. Hell, I couldn't even get him to pump my gas, and he's fixing *a friend's* car? I knew I was slipping. I had no business living with this man that I had only known for ten months. I think he wanted me underneath him to keep me where he could control things. But like a fool, I thought this was it and let him sweet-talk me into living together. At least I wasn't a real fool and let him move into my place, which I sublet to a friend just in case. I never let him know that I kept my old place. He would only try to talk me into getting rid of it totally. Although I had a feeling this was a mistake, I wanted to give him a chance. My past relationships were not going to dictate the flow of things this time. He seemed to be moving his life in the right direction so I gave it a shot. Fabian had a job as an accountant for the advertisement firm I worked for. We met when I hired him to keep my budget in order for a major client I had just acquired. I had heard around the office that he was getting the raw end of the stick and not getting any good accounts. So I wanted to help a brother out. We spent a lot of time together trying to get everything just right. After many late night meetings and dinner parties, we became very close. I thought he was a big flirt when I first met him and I proved myself correct along the course of our working relationship. I always told myself not to let business mix with pleasure, but his charm was too irresistible. So after many months and women later, here we are. I let a lot of stuff go and thought everything would work out. Of course it never did and things began to take a turn for the worst. The other night after some heavy drinking between Fabian and his friend Dennis, I was finally finding out the real story behind the smooth talking people person. Dennis had too many Long Island Ice Teas and started teasing Fabian about where he learned to bullshit people. Dennis kept beating around the bush and making off the wall comments like "Fabian really enjoyed the movie Duece Bigelow", and "Is Black Chippendales on your resume?" He was really frustrating me because by then I wanted to know what was up. Through the course of all the double talk, I finally put together what he was talking about. Dennis and Fabian had been male prostitutes to pay their way through college. Now I have heard of women stripping for tuition, but it seemed like a hard one to swallow thinking of my man fucking his way through school. At first I was beginning to be okay with it until Dennis started saying how the man that taught them everything they knew introduced them to a way to really bring in the money. Fabian was too drunk to even realize that Dennis was telling me the things that he had worked so hard to keep a secret, things that would turn everything between us upside down. He just sat there smiling and turning up the glass of Crown Royal that seemed to be glued to his hand. I was hanging on to every word that Dennis spoke and I felt my stomach begin to turn as he told me of the many nights he and Fabian spent jacking off for some old white man or letting men rub their penises for money. Dennis went on to say that they danced for men at gay gatherings because that was where the real money was. He said that they would leave the function and find some girls that would go along with anything they wanted to do. They would have rough sex with the girls, punishing them for what they had just done. They felt as if that proved their manhood and justified what they were doing. I couldn't bear to hear anything further. I ran to the restroom and threw up at the thought of Fabian and another man enjoying the same pleasures that I had often rushed home for. Pleasures that I had never felt with any other man because of the extreme satisfaction Fabian gave me. I always wondered why Fabian would not leave me alone with Dennis when we were together. I thought he was just jealous of Dennis and his many advancements. But he was just afraid that big mouth Dennis would let the cat out of the bag as he did that night. I could still feel the tears that had stained my face as I took a cab to my friend Simone's house. Simone just cradled my face in hers. The next day we went over to Fabian's to get all of my belongings. Needless to say he was just coming out of his stupor begging me to understand. But for this, there was no understanding. I could understand him lying all those times about the many women, but this time with the threat of AIDS so great, with my life at stake, there was no understanding. Yes, he could have easily contracted AIDS from one of the women he messed with, but dealing with men, I felt like the risk was a thousand times greater. The Michael Jordan wannabe was absolutely right; he had me fucked up in the head. So there I was, storming out of the bar with a vengeance for all men because of the one man whose only defense for ruining my life was the fact that 'I knew he was not gay' and 'he only belittled himself to get through school'. Boo motherfucking Hoo! "I must be slipping! How could I have let myself fall into the trap? No more girlfriend, Love don't live here anymore!" I exclaimed as I got into my Range Rover and headed toward Simone's loft apartment once again. Simone lived downtown so the ride from Buckhead wasn't that long. She buzzed me up and left the door open so I could walk in. "I thought you were going to be slumming all night down at Mick's?" "Guess" I said as I gave her that "somebody blew that" look. "Scrub?" "Uh-huh, and he didn't even look good. How many times we gotta tell brothers that bald heads ain't for everybody." I kicked off my shoes and plopped down on the couch. "Girl you know they all wanna be like Mike!" She giggled and went back into the kitchen. "What you in there cooking, it smells good." "Don't even try it Miss Thang, you know Shawn is coming over tonight. You need to let him hook you up with his frat brother, and get that Fabian off your mind." Simone leaned from behind the kitchen divider to see the expression on my face. I just sat there and didn't say anything. I could not help but to think of what the guy at the bar had said to me and to wonder what in the hell I was going to do now. "You know I was kidding Maxi, you need to lighten up." "I know. It's going to take some time. I damn sure ain't trying to get with anybody now. I think I am just going to go home, I'll call you tomorrow, we'll do lunch or something." I slipped my shoes back on and gave Simone a hug. "Thanks for always being there for me Simone, I really appreciate that." "Don't go feeling sorry for yourself, you know you got it going on too good to let a man make you doubt yourself. Next week you'll have somebody's son running after you and you'll be singing a whole 'nother tune." "We'll see," I said as I walked out the door, "We'll see." It was easy for her to say that. Simone didn't ever have to worry about man problems. She seemed to always find a good one and then dump him because she wasn't comfortable in the relationship anymore or some other crazy reason. She never had a guy do any wrongs to her or even break up with her. I think she was scared to settle down. She would never let any guy get too attached to her or vice versa. Now, she has been going out with Shawn for a while and he really seems to be in love with her. I think he is the one she is going to stay with because she actually seems to match him perfectly. Shawn Alexander stands six foot five with very broad shoulders. His skin has a dark skinned complexion that makes him look like he's from the Islands. He has smooth hair that he always keeps cut and lined up. I have never seen him without looking like he just left a GQ photo shoot. He was so fine that the model Tyson Beckford would be ashamed to be in the same room with him. I think he works as a consultant at a Finance company. He is a nice guy and treats her like a queen. She always gets the perfect guys to fall in love with her. I don't know why my luck was so bad. I got back into my car and headed towards home. I pulled up to my apartment and looked up at the dark window. "It's going to be another lonely night."

Me, Myself, and I

Maybe Simone was right. But the way I was feeling, I didn't want a man to even look at me. I'll just concentrate more on work. I have been neglecting the office ever since Fabian came along, and I made a promise to myself long ago that I would be the best at what I did, always. I have been proud of my accomplishments and knew I had arrived ever since I walked into Smith and Cohen, top floor of the Peachtree Plaza and saw MAXINE STYLES plated in gold on the corner office door. I knew I was good and that it was an honor to have that corner office because of the stares I got when I moved in. I didn't mind because in time I knew everyone would loosen up and we would get along fine. I had never been so proud of my name than at that moment. In fact, I used to hate my name. I never knew that it had the capability to be cute until I had my first interactions with Simone. I always seemed to have a class with Simone all the way up to high school, but we never really had a conversation, just hi or bye sometimes. Simone was very pretty. She had long black hair that was always done and looking good. She had a golden brown complexion that I don't believe ever had a bump on it. And to top that off, she had a nice shape and a big butt. I thought she was a jerk and she thought I was stuck up, so I heard. We were just in two different cliques. But one day, she started talking to me out of the blue at band practice. I wondered what was up, but after Iris, who was supposed to be my best friend fell out with me, I needed someone to hang out with so I welcomed the talk. We just clicked and found out that we had a lot in common. In fact, we became inseparable. We did everything together and were always around each other. One day while we were having one of our usual gossip sessions, my purse fell on the floor and in front of the cutest guys in our class, out pops a maxi-pad. Simone knew I was embarrassed, so she blurted out," Now you see why I call her Maxi!" Everybody laughed, including me and ever since then people called me Maxi. She made light of the situation and saved all of my cool points. After that, I liked my name thanks to my best friend Simone. She always came through for me. And if she couldn't help, I could always depend on my mother. This time I had to come through for myself. Simone was busy getting booty calls and I wouldn't dare call my mother and tell her what happened. I never like to make people's minds up about another person. Besides, her and Fabian's mother became good friends and I know she would be uncomfortable holding that over Mrs. Jones' head. But I did not know what to tell her when she asks what happened. I guess I'll just tell her he cheated one too many times and I gave him the boot. That sounds better than, "I couldn't live with a man that fucked his way through school and may have tossed a few salads for extra credit along the way."

Monday Morning! I hate this slow Downtown traffic. I fought my way to Peachtree Street and pulled into the parking garage. The elevator ride seemed endless as we reached the fifteenth floor. When the doors opened, I felt my heart drop into my stomach. Outside my office sat whom else but Mr. Fabian Jones. "I've been trying to call you all weekend. I really think we need to talk." I looked at the secretary as she sat there looking all in our mouths. "Let's discuss this in my office please." I motioned toward the door and closed it. Cynthia watched us all the way to the door and I could still see her face as I closed the door behind us. "I really don't think there is anything to say Fabian." I laid my briefcase on the desk and sat down trying to hide my emotions. "I do Maxi, you ran out of the apartment so fast I didn't have time to plead my case. And when you came over with Simone, I knew I wouldn't have half a chance to explain." He sat down and leaned on my desk with his hands folded together. "Dennis made everything seem so," "Disgusting and fucked up?" I butted in. "No. Like I had been hiding something." I looked at him and couldn't believe what he had just said. "What do you mean, like you were hiding something, you were hiding something. You were hiding the fact that you have done some foul things in life to make it where you are today. I just cannot see myself with you anymore Fabian. It's not even like this is the first issue that has come up in our relationship, but this is the straw that broke the camel's back. I have been sitting around watching you fuck every woman that gave you a chance hoping that you would stop and things would be good for us again. All of that I was willing to forgive. How long do I have to be your fool Fabian? This shit is deep, too deep for me." He stood up and walked closer to me. "Not this time Fabian, that's not going to work, it is really over between us, really!" "Come on Baby, you know I love you. It's always going to be you and I. Let me hold you and you'll see." I stepped back as if he had some type of disease. "Is it that easy for you Maxi? Can you just throw away the past ten months as if there was nothing between us?" "Yes, and I don't think we should discuss this anymore. If we have to work together fine, but please don't try to think you can finesse your way back with me. I can't be your door mat anymore." I motioned for him to leave. "Are you staying with Simone?" "No. I never let my apartment go. I knew what kind of asshole you were." He looked surprised. "You kept the apartment?" He picked up his coat and turned toward the door. "I can't believe this. I can't believe that you are not even willing to hear me out about this. We were always able to work through things. What the fuck is so different now?" "Everything is different. If you had to hide this thing from me all this time, then you had to know how fucked up it was. Through this entire relationship, the only consistent thing you did was hide shit." "I know that I wasn't perfect. But I want you to know that I love you Maxi, I always will. If this is the way you want it for now fine. But I know you will be back." It took all that I had not to run after him and hope that he would hold me and erase everything that happened. But he was wrong. I was not coming back this time. Tears ran down my face as I sat back into my chair. Even after all the hurt this man put me through, I still found it hard to let him go. Of course Cynthia was at my door knocking as soon as it closed. "Come in Cynt." She swung the door open and sat down with a schoolgirl look on her face. "Is he back on the market or what?" She said as she crossed her legs and looked at me. "Well, if you want him, girl good luck." I pulled my mirror out of my purse to make sure my eyeliner wasn't running. "Perfect as always, but you tripping, that is one fine black man." Cynthia said as she watched me wipe my face. "Like I said, good luck, and why are you all in my business anyway?" I gave her a wassup wit dat home girl look. "Just trying to see who's still in the game, but you know I would never date him, not after you two were such an item." She said as she slid her way to the door. "Yeah right." I yelled back at her while she left my office, no doubt on her way to spread the news. I was sure not up to this mess so early in the morning. I'm glad that it was over, I was dreading the confrontation that was bound to happen here being that he worked two floors down. I felt good. I surprised myself. I had always been fed up with Fabian and his unfaithfulness, and this was my excuse to finally get him out of my life. So cheers to Dennis! Just as I got myself together, Mr. James peeped his head in my door. "Can I see you in my office when you get a minute?" "Sure, I'll meet you there in a few." I wondered what he wanted, surely Fabian didn't go to him and try to quit or be reassigned. That would be a great idea, but he had a good thing going on here thanks to me, no matter how I felt that would not be a smart move for him. I grabbed my planner and headed to Mr. James' office. I knocked on the door and Mr. James was on the phone. He motioned for me to have a seat and smiled. "Yes, she just walked in, I'll call you back." Who was he talking to about me? "Ms. Styles, have I got news for you. Do you remember me mentioning a new account I have been trying to get?" "The one for the Insurance Company right?" "Yes, I finally got to talk to the CEO and he agreed to meet with us. He sounds really young and ambitious, so I want my top person on this one. What do you say?" I was so relieved that he was not talking about Fabian that I didn't even hear him say that he was giving me the biggest account of my career. "Ms. Styles, do you want the job?" After it sunk in what he had said, I jumped up and started shaking his hand. "Of course Mr. James, you will not regret this." "I know, that's why I asked you. Clear your calendar, we are having dinner with him on Wednesday." I was so excited. Mr. James had been talking about this account for the past six months. I knew it was a big account for anybody at the firm. I was honored that he asked me. I had heard that the CEO of Southern States Insurance was a young black guy who graduated from Howard. I like meeting black folk that had it going on like he did. But he was probably some stiff guy who spends all his time in the office. I was so excited that I forgot all about my problems. I guess when some things fall apart in your life, it leaves room for great things to happen. It wasn't a bad idea for me to pour myself into my work. That was the only thing stable in my life these days. I might as well have one love, and if it was going to be work so be it. At least I had control over that.

I'm Fine The Way I Am

I've been putting this meeting off for too long. I might as well get it over with. I heard that Smith and Cohen were the best advertising agency in Atlanta so I owed them that much to hear what they had to say. I just could not bear to sit all night with some stiff executive trying his best to sell me. In fact, I'm tired of being that stiff executive out all night trying to sell. I am tired of a lot of things lately, especially of my mother and my aunts. Everytime I see them it's the same old thing, "When you gonna get married, when you gonna give me some grand kids, it's time for you to settle down, a man in your shoes should not be alone, etc. etc." I'm fine the way I am. Besides, half the women I meet are only out for either the dick or the money, sometimes both.   And the other half are so damn uptight and stuck up that I can't even give them the dick the way I want. None of my friends know anybody good, except for my Frat Brother Shawn, who claims he has the perfect woman for me. If I had a dime for every time I heard that, I'll be a lot better off than I am now. Not that I'm doing bad, being CEO of Southern States Insurance Company don't exactly got me living paycheck to paycheck. Yes, I must say, Justice Dane has done well for himself. But I'm tired of everybody trying to *hook* me up. "Allison, can you reserve my usual table at MoMo Ya for Wednesday?" I asked my secretary over the intercom. Japanese food always put me on top of my game. "Yes Mr. Dane." She replied, and I could hear her writing on her pad. "You have three messages Mr. Dane, one from Mr. Alexander and two from the representative for Posh Advertising." "Call Posh back and tell them that I will not be available until next week. I'm waiting to see how this meeting with Smith and Cohen works out. Thanks Allison." I released the intercom button and picked up the phone to call Shawn. After three rings he picked up sounding out of breath. "Hello?" "What's up man, did I catch you in the middle of something or *someone*?" I said with a whispered voice. "Naw man, I'm just working out. You know I gotta get tight for Simone." "Man she got you whipped. You should be working out to get more honeys not just for one." I said sarcastically. "That's your problem Bruh, you need to settle down and stop sweating where your next piece is coming from. I got convenient pussy, besides, I really like this one man." Shawn sounded serious for once in the eight years I've known him. "Can this be love? Can the bachelor of the year be settling down? I can't believe it, not you man, say it ain't true, say it ain't true!" I busted out laughing. "All that education and status you got and you still 'ignant." "Hey, I can't forget where I came from." "So what you doing Wednesday night? I want you to meet Simone's sorority sister." "Why you always think that if you mention a girl you trying to hook me up with is Greek, I'll go? I thought that this girl was Simone's best friend." "She is, but I want you to know that I ain't hooking you up with no nonsense." He said matter-of-factly. "Greek organizations do allow nonsense in the door, don't sleep. But I can't make it. I have a dinner meeting that night." I heard Allison trying to buzz through, "Shawn, I gotta go, business ya know." "All right man, I'll see you later." "Peace." "Peace." I hung up the phone and thought to myself about the many times Shawn has tried to hook me up, and the many times it turned out to be a disaster.

The next day was exhausting. I had meetings all day and had to hire a new trainer for our east division agents. I thought about canceling the meeting, but then decided to go. I went home that evening and relaxed in the Jacuzzi to ease my tired body. After I got out, I felt better and slipped into bed thinking about the sales pitch that I had to endure the next day. I always thought about work issues before falling asleep. It kept my mind busy and off the feeling of being alone. I finally drifted off until I heard the alarm clock buzz. I got up and followed my morning routine to the office. It was around five o'clock when I received a call at my desk. Allison told me that it was Bob James so I picked up the phone. "Mr. James how are you today sir?" I said in my business voice. "Hello Mr. Dane, I wanted to speak to you about our meeting tonight." "Don't tell me you're backing out on me." "No, I have a family emergency and I cannot make it. I am sending my top agent still. I hope you understand." I thought about telling him to reschedule, but then I don't know when I would be able to fit him back in. "That's fine. I guess if you trust this agent that much, then he or she deserves my time." "Thank you. I will phone you again after I have a report on the meeting." He said with the sound of papers shuffling in the background. "I surely hope that everything is fine with your family." I said hanging up. Well, this is going to be interesting, an evening with some nervous sweaty palmed guy trying his best to keep it together for his boss. And I am not going to make it any easier for him! I loved that feeling of insecurity when these cocky white guys meet me and see who they have to bow down to. I buzzed Allison and asked her to bring in the rest of the day's agenda. Allison was a very good assistant. She basically kept my affairs in order and completely kept me organized. She was a very polite, thin-faced woman in her mid twenties. I never would have hired anyone older than that, I mean, who wants an old hag to look at ten hours a day. The best thing about her was that she was happily married and showed it openly. That meant I would not have to worry about rumors of me dating my secretary floating around the office, and I would not have some lovesick puppy jumping at my every call hoping that I would give her a chance or she had a chance. I already had Wendy, the office skeezer, always trying to strip for me in my office or come in with her tightest outfit on leaning in my face. I know I'm a good-looking brother, but I don't play that at my office. Allison came in with her schedule book in hand and sat down. "All right Mr. Dane, you have one meeting left this afternoon and then you are free until the dinner meeting tonight." She read off the book and then looked up at me. "That's all, I thought I had more to do. Thanks Allison why don't you go ahead and leave, I'm leaving here and going straight to the restaurant, so I think I'll be okay." "Sounds good to me, I wanted to go shopping before I went home. I'll leave your schedule for the morning on your desk before I leave, have a good night Mr. Dane." "Thanks Allison, you too, and tell Paul I said hello." I cleaned up my desk and reviewed my schedule for the morning. I had a meeting at 11:00 a.m. "Good." I thought to myself, "I can have a few drinks tonight and come in a little late."

The Meeting

I arrived at the restaurant a few minutes early, so I decided to have a drink at the bar. The restaurant was a little crowded as usual, they had the best Japanese food in town. The waiter recognized me and assured me that my table was available. I nodded to him and told him I was waiting for the rest of my party. "Whenever you are ready Mr. Dane, let me know." He said as he bowed and walked away. I ordered an Asahi, a very dry Japanese beer and sat down on the stool. I sat on the corner so that I could see everyone that came in the door. I wanted to check out all the lovely ladies that were there and to see how late the Agent would be. I was just about to take another sip of my beer when a beautiful ass woman walked through the door. "Damn!" I said to myself, as this cinnamon skinned sister came gliding past me. She had a small-framed body like a model and just the perfect size breasts. They were palm size, just like I preferred, enough to fit in your hand *and mouth*. Her hair was done in what I heard women call a "curly bob". The length met the curve of her face just perfectly and was tapered in the back. I noticed her nails were perfectly manicured when she reached to her ear to remove her telephone earpiece. She looked like she owned the world. She had a classy walk that made her look like she was gliding across the floor with her fine ass. I liked to see women dressed in business suits, it turns me on, and girlfriend had it going on. She had on some bad ass gator shoes and a tailored suit that fit her oh so well. This was the type of woman that could end up being Mrs. Dane, and that was hard to be. Just as I stood up to walk over to her, she asked the waiter for my table. "Oh shit, this cannot be the agent Bob was talking about, please let me have heard that wrong." "Mr. Dane has not been seated yet, in fact, he is standing behind you." The waiter said as he saw me walk up behind them. She turned to face me and I felt my heart melt. She was even more beautiful up close. She had a beautiful smile that was so warm. And she didn't have a lot of make-up caked on her face, just enough to accent her features. Her eyes were light brown and they slanted when she smiled. "Mr. Dane," she said as she extended her hand to greet me. "It's a pleasure to finally meet you." I shook her hand and smiled back at her returning the greetings. I could tell she was thrown back by my looks, because of the expression on her face when she turned around. "I am Maxine Styles. I'm sorry that Bob couldn't make it tonight, he was so excited about this meeting." The waiter motioned for us to follow him as we went to our seats. "That's all right Ms. Styles, Bob informed me that he was sending his most capable agent to represent him. He has a lot of confidence in you." I said trying to stay professional and not go into mack mode as I eyed her full package. "Would you like a drink before we order Ms. Styles?" I said as the waiter seated us at the table. "Yes, I'll have what you're drinking, if that's all right." I motioned for the waiter to bring two more beers. "She is after my heart." I thought to myself. "Ordering a beer the first time we have ever met. Most women try to front and order some fruity frozen drink that they sip on all night knowing good and well that they are some lushes." She was being herself and I felt comfortable with her. "I must say, I was expecting to meet some uptight guy tonight. It's refreshing to see a young black woman such as yourself being regarded as the top agent in your Company, you must work really hard Ms. Styles." I was trying to see if she had a boyfriend, because I didn't see a ring on her finger, questions like that always get them to tell you everything you want to know. "Why thank you, I must say I was thinking the same thing Mr. Dane, I expected someone very much stuffier." She said as we both laughed. I could not tell if she was interested in me because she avoided the question and was being very professional. I tried to keep it the same but it was hard, this woman was tight. The waiter came back to our table and asked if we were ready to order. "I'll have the sushi appetizer and the MoMo Ya special." She said as she handed the waiter her menu. "You must have read my mind, that's exactly what I order every time I come here. I see we may work just fine together Ms. Styles." She smiled at my compliment and sipped on her beer. I could not believe how much I was digging this chick.

This man was wonderful. I don't know how long it has been since I've met a man like Justice

Dane. In fact, I don't believe I have ever met a man like Justice Dane. I expected to be meeting with this old uptight wanna be white man and here I am having dinner with the finest ass man in Atlanta. He was everything I enjoyed in a man. He was about six-foot five and very muscular. I could tell even though he had on a suit, which I peeped out to be an Armani. You can always tell when a man wears an Armani, it seems to wear them. He also had on the square toe Kenneth Cole's. You could tell he took pride in his appearance and I like a man that looks good and knows it. He had the smoothest light-brown complexion and light brown eyes. His ass fit very well into those pants he was wearing. They seemed to flow just the right way over his hips, advertising he had a good down stroke. His hair was cut low showing off the wavy texture he had. His fingernails were well kept and he had on a Rolex. The mustache and beard he wore was swinging the way they were trimmed so neatly. All his features seemed to be perfect and he knew it. Umm! I hoped he didn't notice how I was checking him out. His arms and hands had so much strength in them that I almost reached out to stroke them. I don't know why I have a thing about arms and hands, but he passed that test. He had a deep commanding voice that had a suave tone to it. He probably could talk you into anything. We were hitting it off and it was like we knew each other for years. I almost forgot I was there representing Smith and Cohen. I decided to clear my mind and stick to business, besides he seemed to be about business anyway. I mean, he was being cordial, but I think that's as far as it is going. A man like that has somebody at home waiting for him, although there's no ring on his finger. "So, Mr. Dane, I would like to talk a little about what Smith and Cohen wants to do for your Company. I think a relationship between our Companies can only turn out to be profitable for both sides." I really meant a relationship between us. "If you don't mind me being forward, I have the proposal all ready if you want to look over it." I took the proposal out of my briefcase and handed it to him. He read the document closely and I could almost see his brain working. I watched him as his eyes ran across the pages. He seemed so careful about his work. I admired that in him, actually, I admired that in any person. I felt close to him and I wanted to know him. I started imagining him moving close to me and putting his arm around me as he read the document. I was just into my thoughts when I noticed him lick his lips. Woo, that shit is so sexy to me. Especially when you can see the dimples in a man's cheeks when they do it. "Excuse me Mr. Dane, I'll be right back." He nodded and returned his eyes back to the proposal. I had to go the restroom and compose myself. "Get it together girl, you are not on a date. This is business and you are not going to confuse the two. But that man is so fucking fine! Okay, okay, I'm cool, I got it all out. I'm going to go out there and represent so I can get this account. Besides, you don't need to be suckered into believing how great he is. You just learned that remember?" I checked my makeup, which I barely wore, you know less is more, and checked my teeth. "Looking good as always girl!" I said as I admired myself in the mirror. I walked back to the table in control. "Ms. Styles, I'm glad to see you back, I thought for a moment you got scared off and left me." He said as he smiled a gorgeous grin. "Never Mr. Dane, do you have any questions about our proposal?" "As a matter of fact, I don't. I have been sitting here trying to think of anything I could question, but as I read on, you covered all of them. I am very impressed with this proposal. I think that we can do business together Ms. Styles." He extended his hand and asked if that was his copy of the proposal. I worked very hard to get that proposal together and it seemed to pay off. We shook hands and talked about the rest of the deal. The food arrived at our table and we spent the rest of the evening talking about the particulars on signing contracts and getting started. We had talked so long, we didn't notice the time. We both had an early start so I paid for the bill, explaining that my Company insisted on handling it and so he offered to walk me to my car. "I would like to thank you for a wonderful dinner Ms. Styles. I hope that we will be working together soon on this project. I have all the confidences in you as Bob does." "Why thank you, I'm sure we will be seeing each other very soon, good evening." "Good evening." He shut the car door as I got in and walked away. As soon as he walked away, I picked up my cell phone and dialed Simone's number. She picked up on the second ring. "Talk to me girl." She had the caller id on and knew it was me. "Girl, I have just met the finest man I have ever seen in my life. I am tripping the fuck out because he is the guy I was meeting for dinner tonight." "The one you are trying to get the new account on?" "Yes, and I want him, damn I want him." "You know you can't do that girl, that's trouble. Look at you now, dodging Fabian in the halls." "I'm not stupid. I don't even know if he was interested. It would have been nice to taste that though." "See, the other day you were through with all men, now look at ya, calling me up 'cause some man got ya stuff wet." "Eeuuw, you so nasty, I didn't even say all that." "Then why you on my phone heffa, come on over. I know you on the way." "Bye girl, I'll be there in a few." "Bye." She said and hung up the phone. This deserved some down-home girlfriend gossiping. And I couldn't wait to get to Simone's.

A Celebration

"Maxine Styles, the best agent at Smith and Cohen!" Mr. James yelled out as he burst into my office. "I just got off the phone with Justice Dane and he is just as excited as I am. He even insisted that you head up his account. I knew I could depend on you to handle this for me." Mr. James stood in front of my desk like a child on Christmas Day. "Thank you Mr. James, I really worked hard on this one." "Who are you kidding? You're a natural. He said you made him feel at ease and he trusted that you knew what you were doing. We are meeting today with his attorneys to go over the contract. I want you to make sure everything is in order. We leave at three o'clock so I trust you will be ready." Bob floated out of my office and closed the door. I could not believe that I was heading the project. Bob usually does that himself. "Looks like I'm moving on up!" I gave myself a "you go girl" and cleared my schedule for the day. This project meant that the other advertisements I was working on would take back seat and my staff would have to cover them and supply me with reports. I would only be directly involved when a decision had to be made or they needed an okay on an ad. I thought about last night and how wonderful Justice Dane was. I actually was anxious to see him again, even if I was only working for him. This was great because now I finally had the chance to get away from Fabian. I would make sure that he could not work on this with me. I immediately asked that Susan, one of Fabian's rival accountant colleagues, work on the Southern States account with me. After I finalized things on our end, everything was in order for the contract. Mr. James came back in my office and we left for the lawyer's office. "I want you to learn how to handle all aspects of obtaining a contract Maxine. I have high hopes for you and you are going to need to know these things. Consider yourself my apprentice." Bob smiled as we passed through the interstate on our way to Alpharetta. "I want to thank you Mr. James for this chance. I will not let you down." We exchanged smiles and he looked over what I had written up. "This is very well put together Maxine, you are learning already, are you sure you've never done this before?" I was pleased with myself. I guess my life was about to be straightening itself out if I wanted it to or not. We pulled into the parking lot of the lawyer's office and we all got out of the car. "Ms. Styles, so glad to see you again. Bob, how are you? Come in and have a seat we are ready to get started." Justice Dane was waiting for us to be seated and asked the secretary to bring coffee. "Hello Mr. Dane" Bob and I said simultaneously. "This is our contract, I hope you will find everything we discussed last night and the additions you suggested." I looked at him and passed his lawyer the contract. I was kind of nervous. I didn't know if his lawyers would tell him to deny the contract or if further changes needed to be done. Bob just looked at me and smiled as if he knew it was in the bag. I wish I had the same confidence, I don't know why I doubted myself so much. I was about to break out in a sweat from worrying. I don't know if it was my anxieties or what, but I could have sworn Justice was staring at me. "He's probably wondering what type of idiot would come up with such a contract." I thought to myself.

Man, that woman sure looks good today. I went home thinking about her last night. I really wanted to see her today to make sure I wasn't imagining things. I stood there eyeing her to take her all in once again and to see if I missed anything. She had nice long shapely legs. That's what made her seem like she was gliding. She had on another bad suit that was tailored just right for her. You could tell she took pride in her appearance. Her hair had a reddish tint and her curls seemed to dance on her head every time she moved. She was everything I liked in a woman. You could tell she was nervous but she took control of the meeting and was sure of herself. I wanted to get to know her and if it meant signing this contract, I would do it. Don't get me wrong, Smith and Cohen was the best in town and everything I saw, I really liked. But she sweetened the deal for me. I could not let her get away. But this was going to take some time. I don't think she likes to mix business with pleasure because any other woman would have cracked by now. Even though I was not trying, I still gave a few flirting gestures and she stayed professional the whole night. I respected that, so I knew it was going to take a while to get to know her, if I could hold out that long. "Mr. Dane, the contract looks good, if you approve, please sign here." The lawyer interrupted my thought. "Smith and Cohen and Southern States Insurance Company are officially in business together." The lawyer said as he handed both of us copies of the contract. "Now that that's over let's go out for a late lunch." I suggested. "That sounds good." Bob said and she nodded. "We can go to Mick's." "Well Mr. Dane, there's another thing we share in common. I go to Mick's to clear my head sometimes, I love that place." Maxine said as we walked out of the building. I'm really liking this woman. I really am. We all rode in their Company luxury van, which I thought, was very comfortable. We had pleasant conversation as we drove to the bar. She was not shy. She joked along with the guys and kept conversation going. I don't believe I laughed that much in a while. It was not because I liked her so much, but she really had things to say that I actually wanted to listen to. Maxine was too much, I could not let her slip away from me. We had to be together. I had to know her, feel her, and take care of her. I wanted to know her fears so I could make them go away. I wanted to love her and I wanted her to love me. All the times I joked Shawn about being in love, and here I was thinking about loving someone who I didn't even know wanted to be loved. When everyone decided to leave, I wanted to beg her to stay. But I played it cool and said my good-byes wondering when I would have the chance to see her again.

Hello My Darling

Mr. James asked me to go over to Southern States and get some information and history on the Company. He wanted to get started on what kind of angle we were going to take on advertising for insurance. "See if they had any prior advertisements or jingles. Maybe we can rework them or make them better." "Okay, I'll tell Cynthia to send all my calls to Nathaniel until I get back. He can handle my other projects while I'm gone." "That reminds me, I want to make an official acknowledgment to everyone that your status here has changed. They need to know you are the boss now. I'll get Cynthia to make me a list of your project workers, you will still work with them, but they have to know, you're the boss now. Congratulations Maxine." Bob made me so happy when he said that. Instead of shaking his hand I hugged him. "I'm sorry Mr. James, I'm just so excited." "No need to apologize, you deserve it, and from now on, call me Bob." I raced to my office and almost exploded. My career was finally rocketing off. I was on my way. "Now all I need is a good man." I said to myself. Speaking of which, I was going to get the chance to see Justice again. I had a good time last night. I wonder if he likes me. He seemed to be flirting with me last night, and I caught him checking me out. The phone rang, as I was about to walk out the door. "This is Maxine." I answered. "Why haven't you called me Maxi. You know I wanted to know how things went for you." It was Simone, I forgot to call her and fill her in. "Girl, I got the promotion! And I am managing the account myself." "Agghh!" Simone screamed on the other end, "I knew you would get it." "Girl, I gotta go, I'm on my way to Mr. Dane's office. I'll call you later." I actually wanted to gossip with Simone and tell her more about Justice, but I didn't want to jump the gun and think he was interested in me. I got in my jeep and headed to his office. On the way over all the love songs seemed to be playing on the radio. I just cut it off and tried not to think of the "L" word. I reached Southern States parking garage and went up the elevator. I got off the elevator and walked into the reception area of the office. His secretary greeted me at the door. "Mr. Dane is in a meeting Ms. Styles, but you can wait in his office until he finishes, it shouldn't be that long." She showed me to his office and I sat down and waited for his meeting to be over. I couldn't help but to check his office out. I was looking for pictures to see if he had someone in his life. His office was very nice; all of the furniture was made with ebony wood. He had very expensive looking art pieces on the walls and statues on columns around the room. I must say, it was very elegant. "Justice Dane has nice taste." I said to myself as my eyes focused around the office. Just when I was about to lean over to see what was on his desk, the door swung open. "Ms. Styles, now I knew I had some beautiful things in my office and seeing you here just confirmed that for me." He said as he rushed in and grabbed my hand, which

I had extended after seeing him. "Why thank you Mr. Dane. I appreciate your eye for recognizing fine things." We both laughed and sat down. I don't believe that I said that shit. But he put it out there and I had to act on it. "And what do I owe the pleasure of this meeting?" He sat behind his desk like he was a king. I almost blurted out, "I've come here for you and I ain't leaving 'till you're mine." "I wanted to know if you had any advertisements in the past and I would like to have a little history on this Company. I want to see what kind of angle we are going to take to start this ad campaign." I took out my notebook to take notes as we talked. "I can get my secretary to give you an old file we have. It's not much, I've never been to big on advertising, but you convinced me to think otherwise." He winked at me and smiled. I swear my mouth started watering when he said that. The tone in voice and that smile! I had to think quickly or I was in trouble. "It's all in a day's work Mr. Dane. I pride myself in my job." That was so corny. I had just been flirted with and that was the best come back I had. It was for the best I guess, because this was ONLY BUSINESS! "Allison, can you bring in the old file we had on advertising suggestions from last year?" She answered him as soon as his finger left the intercom button. "Yes, Mr. Dane." "And arrange for lunch reservations for myself and Ms. Styles." I looked at him and raised my eyebrow. "Excuse me. Would you mind joining me for lunch?" I guess he saw the expression on my face and decided to ask me. It was a nice gesture, I'm not used to a man taking charge of the moment like that. And then again, I was not used to a man like Justice Dane. "Sure Mr. Dane, I would like that." After going through the file that didn't help me any, we decided to go somewhere quick for lunch. "Why don't we just grab a couple of slices of pizza." "Sounds good, I have a lot I want to talk to you about." What could he want to talk to me about? He was starting to make me paranoid. "I hope you don't have any problems with my work. I'm starting to wonder if you are satisfied with us so far." I said as we rode down the elevator to the parking garage. "Oh no Ms. Styles, I just like to get to know the people that benefit my business. Your Company is representing us and you make people's opinion with your advertisements. Do you doubt my tactics?" "I was just making sure. Like I told you, I take a lot of pride in my work and sometimes I think I worry too much." We arrived at a Lexus jeep and I heard the alarm beep off. "Nice car. I like to drive SUV's too. That's why I bought the Range Rover. I like to sit high in traffic. It makes me feel powerful." He laughed as he opened the door for me and we got into the car. "We definitely have a lot in common Ms. Styles." The pizza parlor was only a block away. We got our order and sat down. "So where did you go to school?" He asked as we ate. "I went to FAMU and got my master's at Clark. I always wanted to stay close to home." "So you're from Atlanta?" "No, we moved here in '89 and the place became home. I'm originally from New York." "I hung out in New York a lot. I went to Howard." "So, being in the capital of Greek organizations, did you pledge?" "Of course, how could you not? There's a lot of history at Howard." "Let me guess, you are a Kappa man right?" He laughed out loud and almost choked on his pizza. "How did you know?" "It's the way you carry yourself. All Kappas think they are so suave and debonair. You know, ladies men." "Well, we don't think, we just are. And how about you? Since you asked me that question, I am going to assume you pledged too." He sat back in his chair and put his hand on his chin as he looked me up and down. "Definitely a Delta Girl." "What else is there?" I said as I threw my hands up. We both laughed and ate the rest of our pizza. I was shocked to find out that he was still active in an Alumni chapter. I had been in an Alumnae chapter ever since I graduated. We really had a lot in common.

Time

"It has been a month already and I still haven't asked her out yet man. I know she likes me, I can feel it. I'm not sure if she is trying to keep from mixing business with pleasure or what. I gotta have her." I rambled on. "Wasn't it just last month that you were clowning me about Simone? Now look at you, a sad puppy. Why don't you just ask her man." Shawn said as we played basketball at the gym. "I still think you should have given me the chance to hook you up with Simone's homegirl. Simone said she is raving about some guy she met too. I guess that's out for both of you. I hope you get it together, you need a partner for Spades! My baby and me gonna spank yo ass! And when are you going to meet Simone? We have been dating for a while now and you two have never met." Shawn tried to dribble pass me as he dashed for the basket. "I don't know, I'm kinda preoccupied right now, but I'm dying to meet the woman that whipped you. But you're right, I am going to talk to her the next time I see her. I'm tired of this school boy shit." I walked over to the bench and grabbed the towel. "Maybe I should call her and invite her to dinner. No. I have to be smooth about it. I need to do something that is going to blow her mind." "Man, you gonna blow your own mind. I've never seen you like this." Shawn said as he sat down beside me and gulped down a bottle of water. "This sounds serious and you don't know anything about her." "That's just it, I don't know anything about her, yet I know everything about her. I know things that she likes because they are the same things I like. I know her interest because they are the same as mine. I know she has three moles on her face, one under her right eye and the other two on her cheeks. I know that she twists her mouth when she is trying to figure something out, and I know that I want to know everything about her. This shit is deep man." "Damn," Shawn said, "It sounds like you are in L-O-V-E. And it's about damn time." Shawn slapped me five and drank some more water. "You know what you gotta do. And hurry up, we can start to hang more now that you are going to have a woman. You know single men are hard on a brother that has a committed relationship. You gotta hang with guys that got the same thing going on or you get in trouble." "Yeah, that would be cool. Well, I'm going to head on out. Good game man." "A'ight I'll get up with you dog." I went home and racked my brain about what I was going to do to ask Maxine out. I wanted it to be smooth. I had to meet with Bob tomorrow at his office so I knew it had to be then. I decided to just ask her. She was probably tired of old come on lines and tricks. A woman like that has been hit on in every angle. And I know she probably would turn you down in a heartbeat. Never the less, originality always wins. I went to bed thinking about her and how excited I was.

The next morning I raced through most of my meetings. I barely heard anything that went on in any of them. I was only thinking about going to Smith and Cohen. The meeting with Bob went pretty quick as well. I told him that I wanted to stop in and say hello to Maxine on my way out. He walked ahead of me and caught the elevator. I must admit, I was actually nervous. I walked up to the door that read MAXINE STYLES and imagined that it read MAXINE DANE. Everyone was on his or her way out of the office so I decided to knock softly to avoid any attention. "Come in." Her sultry voice sung from behind the door. "Maxine, I hope I'm not interrupting you." I said as I eased into her office from behind the door. "Of course not Justice, your meeting with Bob is over this soon?" She stood up from her desk and motioned for me to have a seat. Over the month I've known her we had come to be on a first name basis. "Yes, we were just going over a few campaign issues." "I hope everything is going according to your liking." She said with concern on her face. I stood up again and walked toward the window, which had a great view of downtown. "Actually Maxine, everything is to my liking. I cannot be any more pleased." I turned toward her, "As a matter of fact, I can be more pleased. I will be pleased if you were to join me for dinner tonight. I want to cook something nice for you at my place, if you don't mind me being so forward." She stood there with her mouth hanging for a brief second. "Justice, I, I," She straightened her jacket as if to compose herself and continued, "I would love to, do you mean this as a date?" "Well, I don't invite business to my home Ms. Styles." I walked over to her and grabbed her hand. "We have known each other for about a month now and I have been very attracted to you. I didn't know if you felt the same, so I never approached you. I think my timing is right. At least I hope my timing is right." I bent down to look into her eyes." Your timing couldn't be more right. I have to be honest with you Justice, I have been looking forward to this moment for a long time." "Well I'm glad that's out. Would you like for me to send a car for you or will you need directions?" I said with a deep sigh, glad that she didn't turn me down. "You can give me directions, I think I can find the way." I let her hand go and wrote down the directions. "I hope to see you around eight. That will give me time to get home and prepare something for you. I live in Fayetteville, I hope you don't think that's too far." "That's fine. I love the houses and the scenery in Fayetteville, but I thought you lived in North Atlanta for some reason." "No, I hate all that traffic. Speaking of traffic, I better run if I am going to make it home in enough time to whip up something for you. I'll see you later." I touched her on her chin and walked out the office. I was finally about to get the chance to be with the woman whom I felt was my soul mate. The traffic wasn't as bad as I thought. I got home and quickly showered. I put on my "Sweet Nupe" gear that made me look suave and debonair. I laughed as I thought about what Maxine had said before about Kappas. I always kept some type of meal on hand for entertaining, so I knew my freezer was stocked. I defrosted some shrimp and catfish. I put THE TOUCH on them and made a tossed salad. I was so glad I decided to let my mom teach me how to cook, women loved that stuff. And with me planning to always be a Bachelor, I had to have an edge. I put a bottle of wine in the freezer to chill and went into the entertainment room to pull out my best selection of "mood" music. Of course I pulled out Jill Scott, Brian McKnight, Musiq Soulchild, Alex Bugnon, and two mixed jazz c.d.'s. I put them in the automatic disc changer and dimmed the lights. She was going to be mine tonight.

Pinch Me

As soon as he left my office I screamed. "I can't believe this. I can't believe this!" I yelled as I plopped back in my chair. "I thought I was tripping all this time thinking that he wanted me and he does!" I said to myself looking at my reflection in the window. I had a feeling that he was interested in me since we first met, but I didn't want to be wrong. I collected all my files, shoving them in the file cabinet. I raced out of the office and rushed the elevator all the way to the garage. I hopped in my car and started the ignition. I had a big Kool-Aid smile on my face the whole ride singing every tune that came on the radio. I got home and rushed to my closet. "What in the hell am I going to wear?" I pushed through the racks of clothes like a mad woman. I found a khaki silk tunic shirt and pant set that I knew I looked good in. It flowed on my body well and looked good against my skin. I bought it on a trip to New York from a DonnaKaran store. I jumped in the shower and rushed to wash up. I had just got my hair done, so all I had to do was spray it with oil sheen and go. I put on a little lip-gloss and eyeliner and brushed my face with a little powder. "Looking mighty DELOVELY girl!" Yes, I was delightful and lovely at the same time. I splashed on some perfume. It was a quarter to seven so I decided to head out for my destiny. The traffic was a little heavy through downtown to 75 south. I thought I was going to be late as my attention shifted toward Evander Holyfield's house. "He got a guard post in front of his house?" I said as I rubber necked to see the gate. "Probably trying to keep out all them baby mama's he got." I turned into the Country Lake subdivision and followed the directions to his house. Justice had a beautiful home. I could not believe the landscaping. "All this house and he lives alone." I said as I parked in the lighted driveway. I walked up to the front door and rang the doorbell. Justice came to the door looking good enough to eat. He had on lounge pants and a simple mock neck shirt that accented every muscle in his chest and arms. I knew this man had a body, but through those suits I could not tell he had a body like this. "Good evening Maxine, you are looking very lovely. Come in." The inside of the house was just as immaculate as the outside. He had African art everywhere and you could tell he had an interior decorator come in and fix the place up. "This is beautiful." I said as he closed the door. "Like I said, I enjoy beautiful things." He grabbed my hand and kissed it with the softest lips I have ever felt. I could feel my face turn bright red. "Let me give you a quick tour." He showed me around the house, which had columns, silk flowers, and trees accenting every room. All of the walls were decorated with wallpaper and art. The bedrooms were furnished as if they were all occupied. And every window in the house had designer drapes. He had soft music playing on an intercom system that just set the mood off. "Let's go into the dining room and eat, if that's fine with you." He led me toward the dining room, which was lit by candles. This man knew how to treat a woman. "Everything smells so good, where did you learn how to cook?" I sat down as he pushed my chair underneath me. "Just watching my mother. I enjoy cooking. I have to, I enjoy eating." We made conversation through dinner talking about where we grew up and our families. I helped him clear the dishes and straighten up. After we finished, he poured more wine into our glasses and we went into the room where the music was playing. I was really enjoying the evening. He turned the music up and we danced for a while, playing around. He was a pretty good dancer too. My mind drifted and wondered if he made love as well as he danced. I was feeling light headed from spinning around after drinking all of that wine. We sat down on the couch and he turned toward me. "I have been waiting for a month to ask you on this date Maxine. I don't know how you feel, but I have wanted to be with you since the first time I saw you. I already feel like I've known you for years, but I really want to know you, I want to be with you, and I hope you want to be with me." He came closer to me as he spoke. I felt like I was dreaming. "I want to start seeing more of you Maxine. What do you think about that?" "I think that would be fine Justice, but what about work?" "Work doesn't matter. The only reason you have been seeing me so much is because I have been breaking my neck to see you." He said with a low chuckle. "This can work, your Company is working for my Company, it's not complicated. Besides, I don't think anything can stop me from being with you. If you say you are going to be mine, that's it. I'm not letting go." He made me blush when he said that. "Oh, are you blushing Ms. Lady?" "Why don't you stop." I said as I hit him on the arm, blushing even more. "Justice, I have wanted this moment for a long, long time. But I have to ask you to take things slow. I am fresh out of a relationship that really had me ready to give up on all men. I want to be with you too, but promise me that you will take this slow, for me." "Baby girl, I will do anything you ask me to do. And don't worry, I will never hurt you. I am planning on us being together for a long time." He moved closer to me and put his arms around my waist. He kissed me so softly that I could feel every nerve in my body pulsating. All of the imagining that I had done about being in his arms seemed useless, because I could have never imagined that feeling. I wanted him to pick me up from the couch and take me to his bedroom. But I did not want to rush into anything. I had to know more about him before I even thought about jumping into the sack with him. Not that I hadn't thought about it many nights, but I couldn't act on it. And besides, I had to find out how he paid for school, you never know these days. "Well, I hate to say it, but I must be going. It's a long drive back to Atlanta after a couple of glasses of wine." "You know you can spend the night here." "Slow" I said as I backed him off of me. "I'm sorry baby, you can't fault a brother for trying. So can I have the pleasure of seeing your beautiful face again tomorrow night? We have a lot of getting to know each other to do." He said as he leaned back on me and gave me a quick kiss. "Just tell me when and where." "You were meant for me girl, you know that?" He helped me up from the couch and hugged me tight. "Umm," I said. "You gonna make it hard for me to leave." "Slow" He said as he mocked me and laughed. We embraced and he gave me a kiss so passionate that it told me everything he felt for me. "I feel the same way." I said as I smiled at him and got into my car. The ride back was filled with thoughts of what the days had in store for MY MAN and me.

How Slow Is Slow?

When I walked back into the house, I felt like calling everyone I knew about my newfound happiness. Even though it was almost 11:30, I decided to call my mother. "Hello?" My mother answered with a groggy voice. "Hey Ma, did I wake you up?" "Hey Justice, what's wrong baby, you okay?" She said with concern in her voice. "Yeah. I wanted to call you and tell you that I have met somebody special. I really like this woman Ma." "Oh Justice, that's wonderful. She must be something if you calling me this late. Where her people from?" My mother always wanted to know where the family of the girl I was dating was from. She said that roots made up personality. And if she didn't like where the girl was raised, she stayed on me about getting rid of her. "They are originally from New York, but they have been in Atlanta for some years now." "Well, I guess that's okay. At least she has some common sense. Southern girls tend to be slow in that department sometimes. How are my grands going to turn out?" "She is beautiful Ma. You know she gotta look better than a model to be with me. Are you serious?" She laughed and continued to ask me how I was doing. "I know I haven't been home in a while. Hopefully I'll make a trip to see you soon. I love you." "I love you to baby. Keep me posted on, you didn't even tell me her name." "Maxine, Maxine Styles." "That's an odd name. But I like it, it has personality. Keep me posted on Maxine. I hope to hear from you soon. And I'll tell your aunts the good news." "Bye Ma." "Bye baby." I hung up the phone and smiled. If my mother said she was going to tell my aunts, then she was pleased with what I told her about Maxine. That was a good sign. I looked at the clock and wondered if Maxine made it in by now. I decided to call her. She picked up the phone after it rang a couple of times. "Hello. I was just calling to make sure you made it home safe." "That is so sweet Justice. I appreciate that. I was just thinking about you." "Oh? Now what could you be possibly thinking about me?" I said with a sexy deep tone. She giggled. "That's exactly what I was thinking about. How much I like to hear your voice." "Well, if you have a little time, you can hear my voice right now." "So what are you doing now Mr. Dane?" She said as if she was inviting sexual overtones into the conversation. "I am sitting here alone in my house wishing that I was holding you instead of this pillow on my bed." "And what would you do with me if I were there letting you hold me?" She whispered over the phone. My dick started to get hard as a rock as I thought about her question. "Umm, if you were here, you wouldn't have to ask." I answered her with my sexiest voice. "I do regret having to leave, but like I said," "I know, slow. But let me ask you one thing. How slow is slow?" She broke out in the cutest little laugh. "I'm not teasing you Justice. I just can't get down like that right now. I have some things to work out with myself. I'm trying to get to a point where I will not let what happened between myself and this other guy effect things between you and I. You understand that don't you?" "Who is this guy? I want to bust him up for messing my thang up like this." "You so crazy. You don't ever have to worry about him, he is long gone from the picture." "I'm not worried. He can't ever be half of what I am going to be to you." "There you go with that Kappatude. Do ya'll ever quit?" "Nope. We are too legit to quit." "Okay Hammer!" She laughed. "But seriously, I can't wait Maxine. I want this to work out between us. I want to be with you girl. That's all I have wanted for the past month. My boy is probably tired of hearing it." "Yeah, my friend gets an earful too. She has been getting play by play from me ever since I first met you." "He's going to be happy, he wants me to be with someone bad, just to play card games and hang out. But Shawn's cool, you'll like him." "Shawn? What is his last name?" She said in interest. "Alexander, why?" "Oh my God. He dates my best friend Simone! You are the guy he has been trying to hook me up with all this time." "What? It's a small world. Now I wish I had listened to him long ago, he has been talking about you for months." "I can't believe this. I can't wait to tell them about this, what a coincidence." "They are not going to believe this. Well, we already have a set of friends. This is working out better than I thought." "I know. This is too funny." She yawned in the phone. "I'm sorry, that was so rude. I couldn't help it. I am so tired." "I'm going to let you get some sleep. Hey, I enjoyed you tonight." I said with a slow whisper. "I enjoyed you too. I guess I'll see you tomorrow night." "I guess you will. Sweet dreams baby girl." "If I dream about you, I know they are going to be sweet." I could hear the smile in her voice. "Be good." I said as we both hung up the phone.

Good Friends

"Girl you will never guess who Justice Dane is." "Who? Is he a drug dealer or something?" She said playing. "No, silly. He is Shawn's best friend. The guy he has been trying to hook me up with all this time is my man!" "Girl stop. Shawn mentioned his name before, but I never made the connection. When did you find out? And when did he become your man? I missed a whole episode here." "Well, we sort of had a date last night and we hit it off." I said in a sly voice. "You better talk to me girl." Simone said with excitement in her voice. "He came by the office yesterday and told me that he had wanted to ask me out for the longest time. I tried to play it cool, but I was like me too, me too." "No you didn't." "And I raced home and got dressed and headed out to his house. He has a bad crib, he lives in Fayetteville and it is hooked up. He cooked me dinner and we danced and talked for a while." I started giggling. "You did not give up the drawers on the first date ho." "No! What you take me for?" "Well what you giggling and shit for? He got you wide open already." Simone laughed. "That is quite all right because he was jocking me too. He told me all of twelve times that he wanted to be with me. I had to tell him to take it slow. I don't want to rush this and it be a mistake." "And what else you got to do? You better go for it and leave that petty mess Fabian took you through alone. You kill me with that Maxi. Don't let one relationship dictate your

51

next. That invites nothing but heartache and headaches." "Why do you always have to preach to me? I'm trying to spread the news about my happiness and you are blowing my high." "Well excuse me for living. I want you to be happy. Just don't throw it away by comparing him with Fabian." Simone was right as always, but I had to take it at my own pace. "I wonder if he has talked to Shawn yet. I was hoping we could get together this weekend." "Yeah. Shawn has been dying to play some spades. I'll call him and see what's up." "Call him on three way, I want to talk too." "Okay, hold on." I heard the phone click and then click back on. The other line started to ring. "You there?" "Yeah I'm here." "Hello?" "What you doing baby?" "Hey! I was filing some papers. What are you doing?" "Hey Shawn." I cut in. "Who is that? Don't tell me I'm busted." "Ha. Ha. Very funny. It's Maxi. I've got something to tell you." "It ain't mine! And you can't prove that it is!" Shawn said as he joked with us. "You are so silly." Simone said as she bust out laughing. "What is it Maxi?" "Guess who I am seeing now?" "They let Ike out of jail already?" "Why don't you stop Martin Lawrence. I'm serious." "Okay, okay I'm sorry. Who are you seeing?" "Just your best friend. Justice Dane. He is the guy that I met. And now we are dating!" "No shit? You know what? Every time we talked, he never mentioned your name. He is all into you girl. That is great. See, I told you I had the perfect guy for you, but no. You wouldn't meet him and he wouldn't meet you. Ain't that funny how shit come around?" "I know.

We were saying the same thing. Talk to Justice and see if he wants to get together this weekend. We can finally play some spades baby." "Okay, let me go. I'm trying to get out of here." "You coming over before you go home, I miss you." "Of course. You know I miss you too." "All right, all right. Don't forget I'm on the phone. I don't want to hear all that mess." "Well don't listen. I'm on my way." "Bye honey." "Bye Shawn." The phone hung up and I heard Simone back on the line. "I am so happy for you, and for us. We needed some good friends to hang with. And all of us are best friends, this is so perfect." "I better go too. I've been in this office all day catching up on stuff. I'm seeing Justice again tonight. I need to go home and freshen up." "Don't hurt nobody girl." I hung up the phone and turned my chair to the front of my office. I almost fell on the floor when I turned around and saw Fabian standing in front of me. "What the hell are you doing in here? You scared the shit out of me. How long have you been standing there?" I said as I noticed the distant look in his face. "Long enough to hear that you are seeing somebody now. It hasn't even been a month yet, and you are already going out with somebody?" "That is none of your business. We are through and nothing is going to change that. Now if you will excuse me, I have plans." I tried to walk past him and he grabbed my arms and pulled me close to his face. "This is not over Maxi. I am not finished with you. What is your problem? How long have you been fucking this guy?" With every word he said he shook me and tightened his grip. I tried to get free, but he had a tight grip on my arms. "Like I said, that is none of your business. I suggest that you let me go." "Or what? What are you going to do, huh? I want to know what is going on here." I had never seen Fabian act like this. He was starting to scare me. He had a weird look in his face. He was probably drinking before he came in my office. "Look Fabian, things were never right between us. Why are you tripping on me now? You never really wanted me or wanted a lasting relationship. You have fucked so many women since we were together that I have lost count. Just let it go, it is over. Don't make this any harder for yourself here at work." "Oh, because you got a promotion you think you are the boss? Are you threatening my job?" He squeezed me again. "Fabian!" I screamed. "Let me go!" He tried to force me to kiss him and his lips smeared across my face as I turned wildly. He kept pulling me closer to his body and forced his tongue between my lips. He loosened his grip on one of my arms to try to put his hand down my blouse. I was able to push his hand away with my freed arm. Just as Fabian was about to force my blouse open, the janitor opened the door. "Is everything all right Ms. Styles?" Fabian dropped his grip and turned toward the door. I fixed my blouse and moved away from him. "Yes Fred, I was just about to leave." I looked at Fabian and grabbed my briefcase. "Good night Fred, thanks for getting rid of the garbage." I hurried toward the elevator and got in. I kept pressing the button so it would hurry and close. I was a bundle of nerves until the doors closed. "That motherfucker is crazy!" I said to myself as I fumbled through my pocketbook searching for my car keys. I jumped into my car and locked the doors. Just as I was pulling out, Fabian came running out of the elevator. I could see him standing there waiving his arms for me to stop in my rearview mirror. He was running to his car when I lost sight of him. I arrived at my apartment and ran inside putting the chain on the door. I threw my keys on the table and jumped as the phone rang. I picked up the phone hoping that it was not Fabian. "I want to come over and talk." "If you do not leave me alone, I am going to file for a restraining order. That will make a lot of trouble for you at your job. Leave me alone and I will forget all of this." I said screaming into the phone. "I am on my way over there and I dare you to call the police. We are going to finish this and you are coming back home with me." "You try it Fabian and you'll get more than just locked up. I got something for you!" I hung up the phone and went into the bathroom to look at the bruises on my arms. The phone began to ring again. I picked it up and hung it up quickly as I heard Fabian's voice on the other end yelling that it wasn't over. As soon as I walked out of the kitchen, it rang again. I went back into the kitchen and grabbed the phone. "Stop calling me motherfucker!" I yelled into the phone. "Maxine, what's wrong? What happened?" I heard Justice's voice on the other end and I started to cry. "Baby, what's wrong? How do you get to your apartment? I'm on my way." Justice said with desperation.

"No, No. I'm okay. I'm on my way to your house. I'll see you in thirty minutes." "You okay? What happened?" "I'll see you in a few Justice." I hung up the phone and went into my bedroom to pack a few things for the weekend. I changed into some sweats and stuffed my things in an overnight bag. I did not want to stay at my place alone. I knew Justice wouldn't pressure me into anything and I was not staying around for Fabian to cause a scene. I put my stun gun in my pocket and I looked out of my window searching for Fabian's car. The parking lot was clear, so I ran out of my apartment and jumped back in my car. As soon as I tried to close the door, Fabian reached in and pulled me out of the car. "I told you that this was not over." I began to scream and Fabian covered my mouth, dragging me to the back of my building. He pushed me up against the wall making my back slam into the bricks. I was stunned. "Where are you going? Running to your new boyfriend so he can fuck you?" He moved closer to me as he spoke. He put his hand around my throat and put his face in mine. "Fabian please don't do anything you are going to regret." "Shut the fuck up." He said very slowly. "You are not leaving me now Maxi. We are going to make up and everything is going to be normal again. You got me out here acting like I'm crazy. We have to fix this." He tightened his grip around my throat just barely choking me. Tears began to roll down my face. "Shh. I'm going to make it right." He began to kiss me forcing his tongue in my mouth. He pushed his body against mine making the wall press harder into my back. Then he pulled my shirt and bra up over my breast exposing them. He rubbed his face in them and kissed them. I tried to reach my pocket without him noticing, but I could not. He unfastened his pants and looked me in my eyes. "Remember when we used to make love like this outside? I thought this would make you remember your love for me. You used to love for me to hold you by your neck." He loosened then tightened his grip around my neck. "You liked for me to feel you and ease myself into you. I'm going to bring you that pleasure so you'll remember us." He slid his hand in my sweat pants and found his way to my vagina. "Umm, I miss the way this feels." He said as he slid his fingers around it." He pulled his fingers out when I struggled and then he put them in his mouth. "You still taste good. You want me to taste you don't you?" He dropped to his knees and tried to pull my sweat pants down. I finally had a chance to reach my pocket and I grabbed my stun gun. I touched him on the arm with it and he fell out on the ground. "You fucking bastard!" I yelled as I kicked him in the side. I felt his pulse on his neck to make sure he was alive. I then pulled down my shirt and ran to my car. I could not believe what just took place.

It's On

I didn't know what to think. I kept pacing the floor back and forth looking out the window at every car I heard passing by. What could have happened? I looked down at my watch every five seconds. "She said thirty minutes, where is she?" I was about to go nuts. Finally, her car pulled up in the driveway. I ran outside as she got out of her car. I could tell she was shaken up pretty bad. She had a small suitcase with her and I knew something serious had happened. "What's going on Maxine? Why do you have your bags packed? And what the hell happened to your arm?" I lifted her arms as I noticed how bruised they were. She fell into my arms and began to cry. I closed her car door and led her into the house. I got some tissue and let her gather herself. "I was at the office and my ex-boyfriend attacked me." "Did he hurt you? Did he do anything to you?" My heart was racing. I wanted to find this guy and beat his ass. "No. He just grabbed my really tight. When you called, I thought it was him again. I'm sorry for all of this." "Sorry for what? He is the one who's going to be sorry. What is his name?" "Fabian Jones. He works in my office. I think he is going to leave me alone now. I told him I was going to the police. Do you mind if I stay here tonight?" "Of course not. Did he try anything with you?" "No. The janitor came in and rescued me. Leave it alone. I can handle this." She seemed to be hiding something else from me but I didn't push it. "I will leave this alone now Maxine. But if he does anything else, even if he calls you again, I'm getting involved." I pulled her close to me and held her. I knew he did try something with her because her shirt was stretched out of shape. She said he attacked her at the office and I knew she never would be dressed like this at the office. And when I went to hold her, she jumped when I touched her back. Old feelings started to build inside of me. I felt like fucking him up. I had to calm down. I have too much to throw away on some bullshit. I knew that if he raped her she was not the type to just let it go, so I eased up. "Let me make you something to eat and pour you a stiff one." "Thanks. I need one right now." She slid her shoes off and lay down on the couch. I went into the kitchen and poured her a glass of Courvosier. She took the glass and took a hard gulp. "Can I have another one?" She asked as she handed me the empty glass. "You better slow down girl. I might take advantage of you." I smiled as I took the glass. "I might take you up on that. What are you going to make?" She quickly changed the subject. "I'll whip something up." I poured her another glass and handed it to her. "Take that one slow." I went back into the kitchen and made some pork chops and spinach. We sat down at the table and she thanked me as she shoved the pork chops in her mouth. "This is so good." She said as she wolfed down the food. "Don't choke." I said as I watched her eat. "I have a lot on my mind. I hate that this spoiled our evening." "Our evening is not spoiled. I am enjoying watching you act like a drunken homeless person who hasn't eaten in two weeks." She laughed and put her dishes in the sink. "How about another drink." She went into the entertainment room and sat down. I poured two glasses of Courvosier and followed her into the room. I turned on the music and sat beside her. She rose up on the couch and let me slide underneath her. She lay between my legs and let out a deep sigh. "I never would have thought him to flip like that." "Some guys can't handle rejection. I don't know how I would act if you left me." "You are so sweet. I am going to handle this, don't worry." "Let me know if you need me. Don't ever keep anything from me because you don't want me to get involved. I can't let you get hurt." "I won't. I will let you know if anything else goes down. I told Shawn about us today." "I know. I talked to him earlier. We are going to get together this weekend if you're up to it." "I'll be fine." I picked up the remote control and switched the C.D. The smooth vocals of Eric Benet started to sound off in the house. I turned it up and started caressing her. It was my jam playing, Eric Benet and Tamia singing Spend My Life With You. It was the perfect song to hear at that moment. I started to sing the chorus as I turned her to face me. "Can I just see you every morning when I open my eyes, can I just feel your heart beating beside me every night, can we just feel this way together 'till the end of all time, can I just spend my life with you?" She smiled at me as I sung on. I had a good singing voice and I knew I impressed her. She turned the rest of her body toward me and began to kiss me. I think she felt me getting excited, because she pulled her lower body up and winked at me. She was a good kisser and she got me excited with the touch of her mouth. "Is this the part where you take advantage of me?" She said as she looked deep into my eyes. "I would never do that. If you want to take it slow, that's fine with me. But if you are asking for me to take advantage of you, that's a different story." "I know what I want now. I want to be with you. Make everything right for me Justice." She pulled her body on mine and began to take her shirt off. Her skin was so smooth, and felt so soft as she revealed what I had been imagining about and admiring ever since she walked into the restaurant that day. Her breasts were perfect as they plopped against her skin when she pulled her bra off. Her nipples were dark and made a perfect circle on her skin. I wanted to grab them and suck the shit out of them. She then began to pull off my shirt and kissed on my chest breathing heavily. My head was telling me to go ahead and dick her down, but my thinking head told me that this wasn't right. I grabbed her hands and looked at her. "You do not have to do this Maxine. You don't have to prove anything to me because you're upset. I am in love with you. I'm not going to do anything to hurt you. Slow down, I want you when you are ready for me to have you." She lowered her head and began to cry again. "I'm sorry, I don't know what to do. I am so fucked up in the head right now." I put her shirt back on her and led her into my bedroom. She sat on the bed sobbing. I went into the bathroom and ran water into my Jacuzzi tub. I poured in some bath salts and put out a towel for her. "I am so embarrassed Justice." "Shh!" I said as I took her shirt off again and threw it on the chair in the corner. She seemed unsure as I reached to take her pants off. "Trust in me baby, please." She loosened her legs and I slid her panties off as well. By then I was rock hard. As I slid her panties off, I thought to myself, "This is the part where I hit the skins." The hairs around her womanhood were well groomed as every hair curled around itself ending in a perfect "V". She had a cute birthmark on her inner thigh. I picked her up from the bed and led her to the bathroom. I turned the sound system on in my bathroom and turned the volume down so that it played softly. She stepped into the hot water and slid into the bubbles. I got a hairbrush out of my cabinet and began to brush her hair as she closed her eyes. She moaned and slid deeper into the water. I knew she was a lot more relaxed. "I'll leave you here so you can have some time alone to relax. Call me if you need anything." "Thank you Justice." She said as I kissed her gently on her forehead. I closed the door and walked out of the room. "I'm going to have to jack off if I'm going to make it through the night. That girl is too fine, shit." I went into the hall bathroom and began to slide my hand up and down over my throbbing dick, which was begging to come out and play. I tried to be very quiet as I thought about Maxine's breasts and my jimmie erupted all over the floor. I cleaned up the mess hoping that she was still in the bathroom. I turned off the lights in the house and took a shower in the guest bathroom. She was still in the Jacuzzi when I finished, so I just put on some boxers and got into the bed. I put a mint in my mouth so in the morning my breath would be fresh. A while later she came out. I heard her turn off the light and walk up to the bed. "Would it be okay if I slept with you tonight?" "Yeah baby, come on over here and get in." She got in the bed and lay beside me. I put my arm around her as we both fell into a deep sleep in each other's arms.

It's Morning

When I awoke, I was in Justice's arms. He had protected me through the night and I felt so rejuvenated. He was still asleep so I slid from under him and tiptoed out of the room. I went into the bathroom and freshened up. He was still asleep so I decided to cook him breakfast. I thought about Fabian and Justice as I made eggs and sausages. I didn't know what my next move was going to be. If Fabian didn't leave me alone, I was going to take steps to fuck his life up. I never wanted it to come to that. I got a tray and put the food on it. I poured two glasses of orange juice and went back into the bedroom. "Wake up sleepy head." I said as I straddled the tray over Justice's body. "Good morning. Did something happen last night that I don't know about? I usually *make* women want to cook me breakfast in the morning, you know, after putting it on them." He said as he smiled at me. "You did do something last night. Nothing, when I needed it the most. And that was better than any night of hot passionate sex." I threw a napkin at him for being smart. "Evidently sweetheart, you don't know who I am." "Whatever Mr. LoverLover. Eat your food." "So, are you feeling better this morning?" He asked as he ate his eggs. "Much better. I want to apologize for how I acted. I was upset and those drinks didn't help any. I appreciate how you handled the whole situation." I leaned over and gave him a kiss. "All right now, I may not be as understanding this morning. You better watch how you kiss me." I leaned over and kissed him again. He grabbed the back of my neck and gave me a pussy-wetting kiss, slipping his tongue in my mouth. "How did you manage to avoid morning breath." I asked as I pulled away from him to compose myself. "Ancient player's secret." He said pulling me back towards him. He kissed me again and just backed away from me leaving me wanting more. "Great eggs." He said as he looked at me, obviously knowing that he had me open. "So," I said trying to act like I wasn't phased by his kisses, "What are we doing today?" "Well, I wanted to go the movies and later we are hooking up with Shawn and Simone." "What do you want to see? I've been wanting to see a couple of movies that are out." "Let's check out both. We have all day." "I'll go call and see what time the next movie starts." I jumped off the bed and picked up the phone. I listened to the times for the theater and decided when to go. "We need to get dressed. The next movie starts in forty-five minutes." "Good, we can make it."

We got our tickets and got some nachos and popcorn. He ordered one drink with two straws. I thought that was cute. We sat through two movies cuddling with each other and enjoying the film. After the movies we headed back to his house to set up for our first evening with Shawn and Simone. "I need to stop by the store. I need to pick up some beer and wings." "Good, I wanted to get some chips and dip too." We pulled into the grocery store and got a shopping cart. "Our first time shopping together, isn't this lovely." Justice said batting his eyes at me. "You are so silly." I said as I held on to his arm letting every woman in the place know that yes, we are together. "Do you want any particular beer?" "Get Corona, and anything else you want." Justice picked the beer up and turned to hand it to me. He noticed the look on my face when I didn't respond to him. "What's wrong Baby? You look like you've seen a ghost." I could not feel anything as I stood there and watched Fabian walking towards us in the aisle. What the fuck was he doing here? "Baby, what's wrong?" Justice said again trying to figure out what was going on. Just as I was about to say something, Fabian walked up to us as if he was surprised to run into me. "Maxine, how are you? And I don't believe we have met." He said as he extended his hand to Justice. "I suggest you get the fuck away from me Fabian." I screamed slapping his hand away from Justice's. "This is the motherfucker whose been harassing you?" Justice said as he pushed me behind him. "First of all, you don't have anything to do with this shit here. I'm just trying to bring a close to this thing between Maxine and I. We were sidetracked yesterday from finishing what I started." "There is nothing between us Fabian. What the fuck is wrong with you? Why are you acting like a damn psycho? It is over, period, end of story. If you keep on bothering me, you are going to regret it. And I am not threatening you this is a promise. You are looking at serious charges now, remember?" She turned around to show him the bruises on her back and arms. "Look man, this is my lady now. I don't appreciate the way you are handling this. Now, if you want me to get involved, keep this shit up. You better be on your way and stop disrespecting my lady." Justice got in Fabian's face and spoke very low. "If I hear about you again, I am going to fuck you up." Fabian backed up as if he was going to swing on Justice. "What are you going to do, fight me?" "No. I am above your stupid ass. You think I'm worried about you? I do suggest that you watch yourself before you wake up and your whole life is fucked up. And believe me when I say, I can make it happen." Justice pulled me by my arm and we walked off. Fabian stood there saying nothing. Justice could fuck his whole career up with one phone call. Even though he didn't know Justice, he got the feeling that he wasn't bluffing. "I can't believe this. I wonder if he has been following me." "Don't worry about that any more. I'm going to handle him. What else do we need love?" "We need to get a bag of wings and some chips." We walked through the store and got the rest of our groceries and left. I was looking around to see if Fabian was still there. He was gone. "Stop looking for him. This situation is taken care of." Justice put his arm around me and we went back to his house.

Monique Lawton

Nothing like 'Em

Shawn and Simone arrived around eight and it was on. We had everything already set up for an evening of cards and conversation. It was our first night together as friends ever since we found out we all knew each other. "Are ya'll ready to get that ass spanked or what?" Shawn said coming through the door yelling. "Yo, Yo!" Shawn yelled to Justice. "Yo! Sweet Nupe! Pretty Boy Nupe! Wassup Phi?" They embraced and gave each other the Fraternity grip. Simone and I showed a little more control as we simply hugged each other to spite the guys. "Oh, ya'll can't get down like us?" "OOO-OOP!" Shawn mocked us loudly and Justice threw his hands up into the Pyramid signal Deltas flash each other. "All right now, ya'll better watch it." Simone said as she waived them off and sat down. "What are we eating? I hope you didn't bring that Sushi crap in here for us." Shawn said. "Naw man, we going back tonight, hot wings and beer! You know how we do." "I didn't know. You know how dignified we are these days." Shawn slapped Justice five. "Just a part of growing up and getting yours." "You know, if your workers and co-workers saw you two and how you act around each other, they wouldn't believe their eyes or ears." "I know girl, it amazes me to." Simone said as we walked into the kitchen to get the food. "Girl, I have to tell you about what Fabian did. He came to the office and caused a scene, pulling on me and telling me that we were getting back together. He started forcing his self on me and Fred came in and had to save me." "What? What the hell is going on?" "To top it all off, he came over to my apartment and pulled me out of my car. He dragged me to the back of the building and try to have sex with me." I said in a whispered voice. "Maxi, did you call the police? He tried to rape you!" Simone said with deep concern in her face. "No. In his mind he was trying to make me remember what we had. I don't feel like it was rape either. He's just desperate right now. I had my stun gun on me and I gave his ass a jolt." Simone laughed. After saying it out loud, I laughed too. It was kinda funny. "Then, me and Justice ran into him in the store." "What? Is that nut following you?" "I don't know. This is getting deep. Justice told him off and said he would end his career if he didn't leave me alone. He better not bother me again." "Why is Fabian acting like that? I have never even heard him raise his voice." "I said the same thing. He is acting like we were married and he can't get over it. He cheated on me so much, I didn't even think he cared. And now he is having problems with letting go. It just doesn't add up." "He just woke up and realized what he had. You basically put him on top at the firm. That's what he is worried about. His free ride has ended and he is actually going to have to pull his weight around there. You know he wasn't secure in that job until you started putting him on deals. He thought he was dealing with BooBoo the Fool and he could make it last until he didn't need you anymore." "Well, it's over now, he better work on his job skills. His sponsorship has ended." "So, is Justice cool?" "Yeah, he said it was handled. I'm trying to get off to a good start with him. But I haven't told him anything about the attack, so don't say anything." "He's a good catch. So, have ya'll done the nasty yet?" Simone said as she giggled. "No! And he is not rushing me either. But I don't know just how long I can hold out." I slapped Simone five and we laughed. "Sounds like ya'll up to no good in here." Justice said as he peeked around the corner. He walked over to me and kissed me on my neck. "Can the fellas get some of that conversation?" "Well excuse us." Simone said as she carried the wings back to the table. I gave Justice a long kiss and he slapped me on my butt as we walked back into the room.

"First diamond deals." Maxine said as she passed out the cards to see who would deal. "Ha, Ha. Looks like this is going to be a good ass whipping." Shawn said as he drew the first diamond. "Just because you dealing don't mean nothing." I winked at Maxine and picked up the cards Shawn dealt me. I had a good hand. I wondered if Maxine could play, we had to shut Shawn up. "All right partner, how many you got?" "Four and a possible." "Yeah boy! Put us down for eight books. What were you saying Shawn? I don't hear ya now. What are you going? Board?" "Fuck you man. Let's see you play all those cards, you gotta come around this corner, I might be cutting." "It's on you Justice." I lead with an ace of course. We were having a good time. Shawn was mighty quiet as every card they put down got cut. "Set that ass baby." Maxine yelled as I threw out the big joker. "Next hand baby. We'll get em back." Simone said as she leaned over and gave Shawn a kiss. We finished a 24 pack of beer and ate all the wings during the game. I thought we were going to end it with us up 450 to 387, but they wanted to keep up with the punishment. I think I was really feeling those beers and the girls were really silly. These were the times that I enjoyed. I looked at Maxine as I sat across from her. She was so fine and I was glad she was mine. "Can we get some more wings out here. And get some gin too." Shawn interrupted my thoughts. "Man, you got a bottomless stomach." "I'll get it, just don't try to look at my hand." Maxine went into the kitchen to restock our party supplies. I watched her walk by looking at her round ass. I couldn't wait to get some of that. "Don't break your neck." Simone laughed. "My girl is fine, I can't help it. We are some lucky guys for you two." I kissed Simone on her hand. "All right now, only my lips get to touch that skin." "Well come over here and touch it." Simone said as she threw her hand out for Shawn. "I'll touch more than your hand boo." Shawn jumped on her and started kissing her all over her neck and face. She screamed and pushed him away playingly. "What's going on in here? I'm gone one minute and all hell breaks loose." "Let's finish putting this thing on them baby." We finished the game and drank some more. Everybody was tore up at this point. We couldn't play anymore. We decided to sit on the floor and talk. Simone and Maxine made some drinks and came and sat by us on the floor. "I am really enjoying this you guys." "Yeah, this won't be the last time. Here's to good friends and good times." Shawn raised his glass and we all toasted to us. When the glasses touched, the liquor spilled everywhere. We just giggled and kept on drinking. "I don't think that we are going to make it home." Simone looked at the clock and looked at Shawn who was pissy drunk. "It's already 4:30 and coffee can't touch this guy." "Yeah man, I am feeling good right now." "The guest room is always ready. You can stay here, you know that. You don't have to ask." "We're not asking. We are just letting you know. I think we are going to retire if you know what I mean." Shawn and Simone got up and headed upstairs. Knowing Shawn, Simone wasn't getting too much sleep anytime soon.

Slumber Party?

"I'll clean up, you can go upstairs." I barely got up and started clearing the dishes. "Are you sure, I can help." Justice said as he helped me get to my feet. "Yeah, I'll just be a minute. I'm going to put the dishes in the washer and clean up all this trash." Justice made his way up the stairs. I put the cards up and threw the empty chicken bones in the trash. I straightened the room back as best as I could, trying not to fall out. I was still in control of my thoughts but I was tipsy. I turned out the lights and made my way upstairs. I passed the guestroom and heard Simone moaning. I couldn't help but to stop and listen. Simone always told me how Shawn knew how to make love. Many times she gave graphic descriptions of the hot sweaty love that drove her crazy. As I stood there listening to him talking to her softly and her moaning his name, my mind drifted to the scene that was going on behind the door. I closed my eyes and suddenly I was standing in front of them watching Shawn palm the small of Simone's back as she straddled on top of him. He was kissing her up and down her breasts, sucking them as they fell across his mouth. I could see Simone grinding him moving her body up and down ever so slowly with her head thrown back. Shawn held her shoulders down as he thrust his dick hard inside her making her breasts slap against her skin. After about a minute of fast strokes, he stopped and began to kiss her in her mouth like a savage. He slid from underneath her and laid her on the bed. Her head was hanging off the bed and her face agreed with the pleasure Shawn gave her. He kissed her down her stomach and reached her womanhood. At first, he rubbed his fingers across her vagina, occasionally sticking his fingers deep inside her. Then, he positioned his self on the bed and in a dog-like motion, licked his tongue across her vagina. In the same stroke he started sucking her and squeezing her butt. He continued to kiss and suck until Simone's body erupted and she rose from the bed holding his head between her legs. Shawn simply released himself from her grip and held her down on the bed. He kissed her in her mouth and at the same time thrust his dick back inside her. This time, he made slow deep thrusts and with every stroke Simone moaned in passion. She begged for him to go faster, but he continued his slow groove. Simone squeezed his butt and wrapped her legs around his back moving her body to receive him faster. That allowed him to go deeper and he couldn't control himself anymore. "This shit is good baby." He moaned in her ear as he began to stroke her harder. With every stroke, Simone became wetter and wetter. I could see the love juices as his big dick slid in and out from between her legs. I could feel myself getting wet as I opened my eyes to find myself still standing outside the door breathing heavily. I gathered myself and headed towards Justice's master suite. I opened the door and the room was filled with candles and soft music. I searched the room for

Justice, but I didn't see him. I walked into the bathroom and didn't see him in there. Now Justice had an oversized bedroom, but there weren't too many places to hide. I was relieved. I figured he probably passed out in the walk in closet and I was too hot to ward him off tonight.

"Looking for me?" I said as Maxine turned around. I leaned on the entrance to my closet and watched her reaction. I only had on some silk boxers and I knew that my body was tight. She eyed me and smiled. "I thought you may have passed out by now." "I can hold my liquor, can you? I mean you are in control of all your senses aren't you?" I said as I walked up to her and pulled her close to me. "Are you sleeping in here with me again or are you going in one of the guest rooms?" "You tell me." I smiled and kissed her. She wrapped her arms around my neck and gave me a passionate, I want to fuck you kiss. I walked her over to the bed and sat down on the edge. "Are you ready for this?" I said looking up at her. "Yes, I'm ready Justice." She pulled her shirt off and I held her close to my face. I began to kiss her on her stomach and she ran her fingers through my hair. As I kissed her on her stomach, I pulled her sweat pants off and she stepped out of her panties. I stood up and walked behind her. I walked her over to the huge mirror on my wall. I pulled off her bra and ran my fingers over her body. "I want you to see the beauty I see in you. I want you to see how I love you." I whispered in her ear moving her face towards the mirror. She opened her eyes and moaned at the sight of her naked body and my hands searching it. I finally made my way to her vagina and ran my fingers across it. I could feel how wet she was and how much she wanted me. My dick became rock hard. I walked around to the front of her body and kissed her roughly in her mouth. "I want you." Cracked out of her mouth as she stuck her tongue out for me to kiss her more. I grabbed her by the back of her head and kissed her again. She continued to moan and squeeze my arms. I looked at her in her eyes and licked my lips. Then, I slowly dropped to the floor and gave her a sinister smirk. I opened her legs slightly and began to feel her. She felt so good and I knew she was going to taste good too. "I want to taste you." I said, as her expression agreed that she wanted me to taste her. I stuck out my tongue and slowly rolled it around her outer lips. "OOH! That feels good baby." She said as she watched me from the mirror. I pulled her closer to me and sucked on her clit, swallowing her juices. She really tasted good and I was enjoying her. She turned me on with the way she moved her body and held me tight. I reached down and squeezed my dick to get the pre-cum all out, which was dripping by now. I slid my fingers across her vagina again and looked up at her to see if she was ready for me. I got up from the floor and kissed her in her mouth. Her kisses were more urgent now, I could tell she wanted me bad. "Take your shorts off." She demanded. I liked that, dominate me. I slid off my shorts and stood before her in all my glory. She seemed to gasp as she took in my sculptured body that I work so hard to keep up. She walked up to me and ran her fingers across my body. "Now you lay down." She said as she pushed me on the bed. I backed up to the top of the bed and propped myself on the many pillows thrown across it. She crept on me like a tiger giving me a wild look that drove me crazy. Her eyes were so sexy. As she approached me, she ran her tongue against my chest, biting my nipples. With every bite, I jumped because it sent sensations through my body. She laid her body on mine and kissed me in my mouth. "I love you Justice." She said as she kissed me again not allowing me to answer her confession. She slid her hand down my body until it came to my throbbing dick. Her hands felt so warm and smooth as she massaged me and squeezed my head. She ran her hands around my balls gently. "Do you want me?" She panted. "Yes." I answered. "Then take me." I rolled her over and kissed her all over her body. I guided my love inside her as she accepted me digging her nails in my back. I gave her slow strokes and kissed her. "You don't know how long I've wanted this." I said giving her deep thrusts. She simply closed her eyes and held me tight. I pinned her arms above her head and sucked her breasts. I stroked her a little faster soaking in her hot, wet vagina. "Look at me." I said demanding that she open her eyes. She dug her nails deeper in my back as we looked into each other's eyes. "Uhh. It feels so good, it feels so good." She moaned and began to move her body with my strokes. "You're going to make me cum." She groaned as I sped up the pace on my strokes. I kissed her wildly in her mouth stroking faster. She moved her body faster and almost made me cum. "Oh, you feel good baby. It's so good." I never said that to any body. Everything felt so right with me being inside of her. Her body started to shudder as she grabbed me even tighter and moaned out loud. "I love you Maxine." I said with her looking at me. I pulled out of her and came all over her stomach. We lay there catching our breath and holding each other like neither of us ever wanted to move from each other. She got up and went into the bathroom and got a towel to wipe us off. She climbed back in the bed and laid her head on my chest. I pulled her up to my face and kissed her. It was an incredible night.

Life Is So Good

I arrived at the office around 8:00. I had a lot of work to catch up on. The biggest account I had was being handled, very well I might add. But I was neglecting the smaller accounts. I wanted to spend time with them and make sure everything was being done to my standards. I knew it was going to be a long day. I sat my doughnuts on my desk beside the coffee and plopped into my chair to get started. I was startled at a knock at my door. Who is here at this hour? "Maxine, what are you doing here this early?" It was Cynthia. "Got a lot of work piled here if you haven't noticed. I'm just trying to play catch up." "Well, with your head so far in the clouds, I was wondering if you knew you had other clients." She said grinning at me. "Now you know that's not true. I've been working on all my cases." "Yeah, whatever." "What are you doing here this early Ms. All in my Business?" "I'm just getting the conference room ready for Alex's staff meeting. He's having one of his top clients sit in. So, have you heard the latest on Mr. Jones?" "Please, I'm not worrying about that idiot. Whatever it is, I don't care." "Word is he is shooting bad. Nobody wants him on their accounts and everybody is talking about how you carried him this far. They want to get rid of him because he tries to bone whoever is heading the account. Everybody is tired of him thinking he is such the Ladies Man. Since you two split, that shit has played out. You know how women are, they

79

want **your** man." "Well, I'm sorry. He is a grown man. Last time I checked, I didn't have any kids." "Gone girl. I have to go, the meeting starts at nine. Just watch your back with him. Brothers like that will flip on you if their back is against the wall." "Thanks." If she only knew, he already started to flip. I ate my doughnuts and worked on my accounts. The office began to buzz within the hour. I busied myself going in and out of my office collecting files. Most of the accounts were fine, but a few needed my special touch. Before I knew it, it was 3:00. Cynthia bought me lunch, so I didn't have to leave the office. I didn't realize how the time passed so quickly. I was staring out of window when the phone began to ring. "Maxine Styles." I answered. "Do you know what tomorrow is?" Simone's voice sang on the other end. "No, but I'm sure you are going to remind me." "Tomorrow makes five months for you and Justice." "Girl, you are crazy. It sure has been five months. I feel like I have been living in a fairy tale. He is so wonderful." "Shawn told me that Justice talks about you all the time. He remembered that you've been together for five months. Sounds like wedding bells are around the corner." "Maxine Dane. Sounds good to me. But look at you, it is going on a year for you. This is a record breaker. You are closer to that dress than I am." "We have been talking about it, we'll see. I just got off early, let's go shopping." "I have been in this office all day, meet me at Phipps." "See you in a few." I packed up my briefcase and headed for the door. I needed a break and I wanted to pick something up for Justice. I drove down the street and found a parking space at Phipps Plaza. Simone pulled along side me after I waited about fifteen minutes in my car. "Hey girl!" Simone said as she hugged my neck. "Have you been waiting long?" "No, just a few minutes. Let's do it." "It has been so long since we had a shopping spree. Where do we begin?" "Nordstrom's!" We both said in unison. "Cynthia mentioned Fabian today." "What is that fool up to now?" "Everybody is peeping him out. I guess I really did put him where he is now. He's trying to sleep his way around and nobody is buying it." "Ha. That shit has run out on his ass. Those type of guys always get theirs in the end." "And he knows about getting it in the end, rear end." "Ooh girl, you crazy." Simone said busting out laughing. We made our way around the stores in the mall. Dipping in and out of boutiques we talked and laughed. I was starting to feel like my life was good, and I haven't felt that way since I was a child. "So, let's talk about you and Justice." Simone said as we walked into the food court. We sat down and put our bags on the chair. "I don't know Simone. I'm scared. Everything is going so perfect, I feel like something is going to happen to mess it all up." "You can't do that Maxi. Hoping for the worst only brings the worst. Roll with it. You are young, you have a slamming career, and you don't have any kids tagging behind you. You should be living high off the hog. Look at me. I had to struggle for a while before I got on my feet. You were my motivation to get through school and become an Investment officer." "I always looked up to you, I never knew you looked up to me." "That's because you are always doubting yourself, always worried about how everybody else perceives you. Do your thang girl." "I'm so lucky to have you in my life Simone. You know what? I'm going to let go. And to celebrate, I'm going to buy something sexy and surprise Justice at his office." "There you go lady, live a little. Let's go to Fredrick's and see what they have." We left Phipps and drove over to Cumberland Mall to see what they had at the store. I always had such a good time with Simone, she was my sister and I felt that to be true. "Get something red and get some red heels, spiked ones. He'll appreciate that." "I can't walk in his office with spiked red heels. Those people know me." "Yeah, you're right, but get them anyway, save 'em for later." Simone chuckled. "You are so silly. I bet Shawn would love to see you in this." I held up a leather cat suit with openings everywhere." "Ooh, you are so right, I'm getting this." Simone said snatching the suit away from me and holding it up to her body. "I can get him to do anything with this." I laughed, but I knew she wasn't joking. That was a whole 'nother Oprah that I wasn't getting into. "Let's just buy the stuff and go, rush hour is about to start up." "It's that time already? Yeah, let's go." We paid for our items and hugged each other as we headed to our cars. "Call me tomorrow after you shock the hell out of your man." "And you too, that is if anything you do can shock Shawn." "Wouldn't you like to know?" "Be good, I'll talk to you tomorrow." "Bye." I drove off to fight with the afternoon rush. I played the scene of Justice and me over and over in my head. That night I could hardly wait to see Justice. I was ready to give my all to him and stop holding my past relationships over his head. I finally found the man for me, and how I felt, he could very well be my soul mate. I had made it up in my mind to not let any of my past failures taint this relationship. I poured a glass of Zinfandel and played some jazz. I plopped on my sofa with my oversized bathrobe and relaxed. I was actually content with my life.

Not What It Seems

I felt odd by not having a conversation with Maxine last night. She has become an everyday routine with me, but I was in meetings pretty late. That made me all the more not wanting to go into the office, but I had to remember that I had a business to run. I felt like I was in high school again and I was girl chasing. But this was much different. I wanted nothing more than to be with Maxine. I've never known this feeling before and it felt good. It is rare that you find a woman that fits all the things that you look for. She completed me and I needed to make her a permanent part of my life. My train of thought was broken as the elevator door opening. Well, I guess I'll get my day started. The morning was going to be filled with meetings and more meetings. Allison met me in my office with a cup of coffee to brief me on my day. The only free time I was going to have was at five when the office would be empty. I hoped that the day would go fast. Today makes five months for Maxine and I. I planned to meet her at her apartment and surprise her. I had my housekeeper fix up my place for a romantic evening. I was going to pick her up and take her to my place to celebrate. Tonight was the perfect night to talk about us becoming a more frequent couple. I wanted to advance our relationship a little further. My first meeting started and then ended three hours later. I had a luncheon to go to next and then two more meetings after that. Just like I figured, it was a quarter to five when I finally ended my last meeting and returned to my office. Everyone was packing up for the day and I had to prepare a few papers and then I could leave. I unloosed my tie and took the stack of papers from my briefcase. As I was just getting started, there was a knock at my door. I thought everyone had left. "Come in." I said wanting to know who it was. The door flew open and Wendy came strolling in looking slutty as ever. "Yes Wendy, what can I help you with?" I said not wanting to deal with this bullshit today. "Well, actually I came by to help you." "With what?" "With the tension buildup. I've noticed it all week. You need someone to help you loosen up a bit." "Look Wendy, I appreciate your concern, but I don't need you to do anything for me, ever. I wish you would stop coming on to me. Do you realize I can have you fired?" "But you won't." She said as she started to walk closer to me. She walked up to my desk and pulled off her dress. "How long are you going to keep saying no to this?" She said pointing to her nude body. "I can make you happy Justice, I can make you feel like a real man." She said as she walked behind the desk closer to me. I was stunned that she went this far, before she just made innuendoes and comments. I never really took her seriously, but here she was standing over me butt naked. "Look Wendy, you have gone too far this time. You know as well as anybody in this office that I don't play that." She straddled over me trapping me in my seat. "Tell me you don't want this." She kissed me on my neck. "Wendy!

85

Get off of me now!" I grabbed both of her hands and tried to get her up, but her fat ass had me pinned down. She continued to kiss on my neck and grinding her nude body against mine. "Tell me how you want it." She whispered in my ear. And as she said that, the door opened. I struggled to look around her to see who it was and how was I going to explain this to my employees. With that thought, I made the figure in the doorway to be the only person whom I could not possibly explain this to. The one person who I wished would have never walked in that door. Just as I tried to get up again, she spoke with painful words. "No, don't get up for me, don't let me interrupt. And please, do not call me to try to explain this shit, just stay away from me. Happy Anniversary Mr. Dane." Maxine turned to walk toward the door and stopped. She turned back around and looked at Wendy. "I guess we had the same idea." She swung open her dress to reveal a hot red negligee that held on to every curve she had. She was looking damn good. "You can have him, I'm through." She said as she turned again and walked out of the door. "Maxine!! Maxine, wait." I screamed pushing Wendy onto the floor. I ran to the elevator door and saw the streams of makeup running from her face, soaked with tears. The door closed in my face before I could say anything. "Fuck! Fuck, fuck, fuck." I slammed my fist against the wall. I went back into my office to grab my things to go after her. "Get your stuff and leave this office Wendy. You have done enough damage here." Wendy didn't say a word, she just picked up her dress and slid past me. I hid my face in my hands and shook my head. How was I going to explain this? The only woman that I ever cared anything about just caught me out of pocket and she will never believe that I never touched that woman. I sat down to gather my thoughts. I picked up the phone to call Shawn. He had to get my side of this to explain to Simone for me. The phone just rang and rang at his office, so I called him on his cell phone. "Yo." "Shawn, you will never believe what just happened to me." "What, are you okay?" "Hell no. Man Maxine just walked in on me with that bitch Wendy on top of me naked." "What? Are you stupid? What you doing fucking with her?" "I wasn't. Man you know how she is always after a brother. She forced herself on me and I was trying to get rid of her when Maxine walked in." "Damn. Aint no explaining that shit." "She will never let me explain. She just told me not to try to contact her. And get this, she was wearing something sexy for me under her dress. She came to surprise me at the office and walked into this shit. She has never done anything like that and to walk into something like that had to fuck her up. I could have killed that damn Wendy. What am I going to do? How in the hell am I going to get past this? All she ever talked about was how guys messed her over and how scared she was to get serious with me. This was a step for her and it's all fucked up now." I said in one breath. "I believe you. I know you better than that. I'll talk to Simone and tell her how it happened. She can talk to Maxine for you. It's good to have the best friend on your side, but I better call her before Maxine does." "Call me as soon as you hear something. Do you think I should go over there?" "No. Just leave her alone for now. Try to call her later, she is probably really upset right now." "Call me back." I hung up the phone and actually began to cry. "This woman got me crying?" I said out loud. "I love her, and I just fucked up." I banged my fist against the desk and collected my things. I had to think about how I was going to handle this. She was very hurt and nothing I could say right now would help. I looked around the office replaying the scene that just took place. "Two beautiful women in my office, one naked the other half naked and I'm going home whining like a bitch!" I said as I turned off the lights. "How did a player like me get to this point?" I walked to the elevator feeling like my heart has just been ripped from my chest. I headed for my house and thought about Maxine the entire ride with tears in my eyes.

When?

I got into my car and drove for my apartment. I could barely see through the tears in my eyes. Why is it that everytime I decide to give myself to a man, I get pissed on? Am I that type of woman that only attracts assholes? My heart had just been stepped on. I can't believe a man like Justice would do something like that. Why would he do this to me? I pulled into my parking space and sat there sobbing. I finally got myself together enough to go upstairs. I walked straight to the bar and grabbed a bottle of whatever was close. I plopped on the couch and took a long gulp of the liquor. "What the fuck just happened?" I said as I gulped the bottle again. I pulled off my dress and the negligee I wore for my love. I threw it on the floor and put on some jogging pants and a t-shirt. I jumped back on the couch and turned the ringer off my phone, which had already begun to ring. "I don't want to hear your fucking lies Justice." I yelled at the phone as the light on my answering machine flashed over and over. I gulped down more liquor and started to cry. "Why is it that everytime I think my life is good something comes along to slap me back into reality?" I finished the bottle and grabbed another one. "Well, good riddance Mr. Dane." I said toasting the air. "Good riddance to the fairy tale." I wiped my hand across my face and gulped down the bottle. I drank two more bottles and passed out on the floor. The next thing I knew, Simone was slapping me and wiping my face with a cold towel. "How did you get in here?" I said slurring my words. "I got a key heffa, what are you doing? Trying to kill yourself?" Simone said pulling me up on the couch. "Why aren't you answering your phone she said as she turned the ringer back on. The phone immediately began ringing. "That's why." Simone picked the phone up. "Hello? No, she's not okay. She just tried to kill herself that's all. She's drunk out of her mind. Four Bottles. No, that's the worst thing you can do, just give it some time." "Hang up on that motherfucker Simone. Don't tell him shit about me. He wasn't worried about me when he had that big booty bitch sprawled out all over his lap." I slurred and started crying again. "Fuck you Justice and fuck me for loving you, you bastard." "She's drunk. I know. She doesn't mean it. Okay. Bye." "I do mean it Simone, I do." I fell into her arms and sobbed loudly. "Why Simone? I love him so much and he is fucking someone else. Why?" I said as Simone tried to get me to my feet. "He said that she forced herself on him and you walked in as he was trying to get her off of him." "Get off? How did she get on? How much forcing can a woman do to a man as built as Justice? It takes time to get your clothes off and get on top of somebody Simone. I don't believe that shit." "Stop it. You are not being reasonable. I'm going to run a tub of water for you. We'll talk about it when you sober up." Simone helped me into the tub and helped me wash up. I just cried and cried uncontrollably. "It's over. It's all over." I cried as she helped me into my pj's. "Get in the bed."

Simone said as she pulled the covers over me. I cried and cried as Simone lay next to me rubbing my head. "It's going to be all right Maxi. You'll see."

When I awoke in the morning, I felt like I had been run over by a truck. Simone was in the kitchen cooking breakfast. "Tell me that last night was just a dream." I said holding my head. "I wish I could, but it is not as bad as you think." She said handing me a plate of food. "Oh no? You tell me how bad you think it is if you caught Shawn with another woman." "I'm not saying that Maxi, you really should give him a chance to explain what was going on. Shawn told me that she came into his office and took her clothes off. He said Justice was trying to make her leave when she jumped on top of him and that's when you happened to walk in." "Bullshit Simone. I just can't bring myself to believe that. It looked as if he was busted when I opened that door. Plain and simple, he got caught out of pocket. I don't know what I am going to do now. I love him so much Simone, and it hurts so bad." I began crying again. "How did I get to this place again? I really think that I am going to become an old lonely woman." Simone walked over to me and held me tight. "He loves you Maxi and you know I don't give any body the benefit of the doubt, but I really feel that he is telling the truth. Why don't you talk to him and see what happened." "I can't. If I look him in the face I know that all I will see is Fabian and Will and Lance and all the other assholes that I've dealt with that did me the same way. I can't handle those feelings again, and that is all that comes to my mind." "That's the problem Maxi, you keep bringing up those idiots. Justice is not like them, this is the man you are going to marry. This is the man that is going to change everything for you and make you a happy woman. This is the man that is going to make you a mother. Can't you see that?" "No, I can't. I cannot see that. All I can see is the hurt that I am feeling right now. The hurt that keeps coming back to haunt me time and time again. The hurt of loving someone that is not capable of loving you the same way. Even if I believe that Justice was trying to get away from her, which I don't, I'm scared that something else will come along to take me down this path again. I can't be that fool anymore." "I know you are scared. But you are going to have to let somebody in. You never truly let Justice in." "I don't think I can. For this same reason, I don't think I can." "You will have to or you will be that lonely old woman." Simone cradled my face and hugged me. I knew she was right, but the hurt was controlling me. I was scared to believe what Justice said because I was scared of the next time something happened. I had no idea what my next step was going to be. But one thing I did know was that it was going to be manless. Simone walked back into the kitchen and cleaned the dishes. "You will get over this child. Just take things day by day." "I am not trying to hear that right now. I feel like crap. I know one thing I am going to do is stop drinking so much. I have to stop letting that bottle take away the pain, because if I have to feel like this the next day, it's not worth it." I got up and ran to the bathroom to throw up. Simone followed me laughing. "Amen to that. That's what you get. Calling Earl this morning huh?" I just rolled my eyes at her and washed my mouth out.

Back?

"I believe I have spent the past two days pacing my whole house. My fingers are starting to hurt from dialing Maxine's number so much. I could kill that bitch Wendy for getting me into this shit. I should have kicked her out of my office as soon as she walked in. But I must admit I must have been curious because I let it go as far as it did. What am I going to do now man?" "That's the trouble with us. That little head has a stronger mind than our big head at times and it gets us in shit. But you should have known that Wendy is nothing but trouble. It is going to take a lot of begging to get back in you know. Simone said that it is not looking too good. She said that Maxine is tripping. She doesn't even want to see or hear from you." "You got to be kidding. I thought ya'll said that if I gave her a couple of days she would be ready to at least talk." "Yeah, but she is taking this harder than I thought." "I can't let her go through this alone. I have to try to see her." I hung up the phone and started putting on my clothes. I didn't care what Shawn thought, I had to go and try to see her. On my way to her apartment, I thought of what I would say, how I would explain to her that she walked in on a situation that looked like more than what it was. I rehearsed my apologies over and over until they started to sound lame. My heart began beating faster when I pulled into the parking lot. I got out of the car and took a deep breath. "Justice." I turned around to see who called me. It was Simone locking her car door and walking towards me. "What are you doing here?" "I wanted to see her. She won't answer any of my calls and I need a chance to talk to her. It's been three days since this has gone down and I feel lost without even knowing how she feels." "Well, I've been trying to put in a good word for you, but she's hurt, you know? I finally talked her into going out with me tonight. She's expecting me to come up so why don't you go and try to talk to her." "Thanks Simone. I just need to tell her that I didn't have anything to do with that girl. You know that I would never do anything to try to hurt her?" "I know, but be easy with her. She is not expecting to see you." Simone gave me a hug and walked back to her car. I walked to the elevator and watched the numbers light up until I reached her floor. I walked down the hall and stood in front of her door. "Please let this go right." I knocked.

"Come in Simone, the door is open." She yelled from behind the door. I walked in and stood in the doorway. "I was just finishing my makeup. I don't know why I agreed to go out with you, this is the last thing I need." She said as she walked back into the living room. I wanted to run up to her and hold her tight. I just stood there and took in all her beauty. She finally saw me standing there and her faced dropped. "You look good Maxine." I said as she just stared at me. "What are you doing here? I have nothing to say to you. Can you please leave." She walked toward the door and brushed past me holding the door open. I could smell that familiar scent that drove me crazy and I wanted to grab her and kiss her. "I need to talk to you." "I have company coming over and they will be here any minute." "Who, Simone? I just begged her to leave on my way up." "Dammit Simone." She said as she slammed the door and walked back into the living room. "Look, there is nothing that we need to talk about Justice. It's cut and dry, let's not make it anything else." "Listen to me." I said and walked over to her. She immediately turned her back. I turned her around gently to face me. "Listen to me." I said forcefully. "I never wanted to hurt you. When you walked into that room, my whole world ended. There was nothing going on. She threw herself on me and you walked in at that exact moment. I..." "How did she do that Justice?" She blurted out with tears rolling down her face. "How can a man who is so damn set on working out and being strong let a woman no more than what, 140-145 force herself on him? Something had to be there to let you submit to her. And that something is the one thing I don't want to be a part of." "Maxine, you don't mean that. I only want to be with you and I have never wanted that with any one else." "Oh, well you sure have a funny way of showing it." Her words were harsh and painful. I never saw this side of her. "Baby, let me make it right." I pulled her close to me and kissed her face. "No!" She yelled pulling away from me, "you can't make it right. I can't let you." Surprised at her confession, she turned to walk away and I grabbed her arm. "Why won't you let me? You know in your heart that I did not have anything going on with Wendy." "How do I know that Justice? All I know in my heart is hurt. It hurts." She began crying heavily and I just held on to her like my life depended on it. "Let me go, please. Please let me go." She buried her head in my chest and cried. I couldn't do anything but hold on to her. "I'm not letting go girl. You here me? I'll never let go." She continued to cry and I pulled her face to mine. "Look at me." I said to her. "Look at me." She raised her streaked face and looked at me. "I love you Maxine, and you mean everything to me. I would never do anything to jeopardize that. We are going to be together and everything is going to be right again." She just shook her head and slipped out of my arms. She fell back to the couch and looked up at me. Just then, Simone walked into the room and over to Maxine. "Maybe you should leave now Justice." She said as she kneeled down to pick Maxine up and wipe her face. She looked at me and whispered, "Give her some time." They both walked into her bedroom and closed the door. I wanted to go after them, but I just walked toward the door turning to look one last time hoping she would come back out and everything would be okay. I left her apartment and got into my jeep. I started up my car and the tears just rolled down my face.

Sad Songs

"Why did you let him come here? I was not ready for that." "I'm sorry, but you needed to give him a chance to explain." Simone wiped the rest of my makeup off my face. "Do your makeup over so we can go." "You expect me to go out after dealing with that?" "Yes, and I will not take no for an answer. Look at you, you haven't looked this good in days." "I'll go, but no talking about Justice. I need a drink now." "You lush, hit this and let's go." Simone handed me a joint to help mellow me out. "Damn, we haven't smoked in ages." "I know, tonight is special, I pulled out my stash just for you." "I hope I don't get tested come Monday." I said lighting up. I was up for anything right about now. We smoked the joint almost coughing up our lungs and then headed out for a club. I couldn't believe that I was going out after that episode. We reached the club and got a seat at the bar. I ordered a drink and looked around at the atmosphere. Before I could take a sip of my drink, the wolves were already out. Simone accepted and went on the floor to dance. By the time she got back, I had three more drinks. "Girl, you better pump your breaks." "Pump my breaks, why? Like I got somebody to go home to." I took another sip of my drink. "So you didn't feel anything when Justice came over?" Simone said as she accepted a drink from a guy sitting at the end of the bar. She knew I was tipsy and that I would tell her the truth now. "Hell yeah. He was looking good. I almost folded. You came in at the right time." "Damn, I should have went home. You need to be with him." "No I don't Simone. I can't trust him. But I do love him, and that is going to be hard to get over." "You're crazy. That's a good man." "I don't know, I'm just in a lot of pain right now. But I think that guy walking over here will help for tonight." I said eyeing this fine guy who was eyeing me. "Don't turn into a ho just because you are feeling down." "Excuse me Miss Thing. You are the one to talk." "Would you like to dance Ms. Lady?" The guy said as he reached our seat at the bar. "Talk to you later." I gave Simone a wink and took his hand. I was feeling a little too good, I was all over the guy feeling on his bulge and rubbing his butt. I danced with him like I used to back in my wild college days. I used to get freaky when I danced and tonight I was reminiscing. All eyes were on me and I didn't care. His hands were all over me as I continued to grind on him. We danced through the next four songs. For a second, I forgot all about Justice and it felt good. I knew I shouldn't have drunk so much, but this guy was taking the reality away and I was enjoying myself for the first time in a while. After the DJ pissed us off and started playing some junk music, the moment was over. He escorted me back to the bar and gave me a kiss on my neck. "Can I get your number Ms. Lady?" He whispered in my ear. I asked the bartender for a pen and I wrote it on a napkin. He looked it over and gave me a sexy smile. "My name is Bryce, I'll be calling you Maxine." He walked away and I turned to Simone. "Don't hurt nobody girl." She said raising her eyebrow. "What?" "You know what. I haven't seen you act like that in years." "Well maybe that's what's wrong with me, I'm all wound up because of my career. I need to let loose." "And what is your definition of loose? You better watch it girl." "Can I have any fun Momma?" We both laughed and sipped the rest of our drinks. "Here comes another one." I said only seeing the shadow of a man approaching us. Simone swung her chair around to look. "Shit! Do you know who that is coming over here?" Before she could say anything, He was standing behind me. "Maxine Styles." I knew that smooth, sultry voice all too well. This would be just about all I can stand tonight. "Lance." I said as I turned to face him. "Funny running into you here." Simone said with sarcasm. "Of course, the tag along, hello Simone. How could I have missed you?" He said giving her a smirk grin. "Baby, you look more incredible every time I see you." He said bending down to kiss my face. Lance was one of the reasons I was so reluctant to give in to Justice. He was one of the guys in my life who tore every bit of self-esteem and self worth I ever had from me. I poured all my love into him and he took advantage of that. We were together for two years and when I was dependent on him the most, he left me for another girl from school. We were back and forth between him deciding he missed me and getting with someone new. He knew what kind of guy women thought he was and he ran with it. "I must say you're looking good yourself

Lance." I could feel Simone getting madder and madder. I looked at her and gave her a sneaky smile to let her know it was okay. "I saw you dancing with that brother. You used to only dance for me like that. I didn't appreciate it. You think I can have this dance for old times sake?" "Why not." I hopped off the barstool and he led me to the dance floor. This was my chance to prove that he did not pose a threat to me anymore. I was feeling a little bold and he was putting me to the test. A slow jam was playing and Lance pulled me close to him like he used to do. "Uhm, you still feel good. I miss this Maxi. I always think about you." I rolled my eyes in my head. Yeah right he was thinking about me, thinking about fucking and that's about it. "Really?" I said as I slowed down the pace and met his thrusts with a teasing grind. "This takes me back. How have you been?" He said whispering in my ear, letting his lips touch with every word. He knew how that turned me on, but it wasn't working this time. "I've been fine, but I see you are still up to your old tricks." "Come on Maxi, I haven't seen you in three years and this is how you treat me?" He pulled me even closer and ran his hands down my back. "I told you I missed you, why is that playing games?" "Whatever Lance." He smiled and continued to hold me tight. "You feel so right being in my arms again. You know you have always been mine. How does this feel to you baby?" "It's a dance Lance." "Cold blooded, I guess it's been too long. You know I'm back in Atlanta now, why don't you come back to my place tonight to talk about old times. You know I haven't gotten over you yet. You are my first love, I will always hold a place for you in my heart." I didn't say a word. I knew the 'I'm lonely and I want to sleep next to a warm body' routine. The song was over and he led me back to the bar. "Thanks for the dance, it was nice seeing you." "See you later Lance." Simone said when I sat back down. He ignored her and continued, "The offer stands." He said holding out his hand. I took it and pulled him close. "See you later Lance." I whispered in his ear, letting my lips touch his skin like he used to do to me. Simone chuckled and he looked at me in disbelief. I turned around facing the bar and picked my glass up again. "You still here?" Simone said laughing and holding her drink up to him. He just walked away without saying anything. "Girl you crazy." Simone was loving it. She slapped me five. "He thought he was back in just like that, Sike!" "I am proud of you. Tonight turned out to be all right." We cheered each other and decided to head on out. "Let me go pee first." I went to the restroom, all those drinks were catching up to me. On the way to the restroom, I felt someone grab me and start kissing me. I was too drunk to resist and when the person turned me around, I didn't want to resist. "Remember me?" Bryce said as he squeezed his hands all over my breasts. I smiled and began to kiss him. He was just about to put his hands down my pants when some sense came to me. "Maybe another time." I pulled away from him and continued to the restroom. When I came out, he was gone. I made my way back to the bar and Simone and I walked to the car. "I'm glad you are driving, I am just about toasted." I climbed into the car and passed out.

Goodbye Yesterday

"I hope you are going to stop moping around the office Mr. Dane. I hate to see you like this." Allison said as she handed me a cup of coffee and the day's agenda. "I'm sorry, it's just been hard to face the fact that it may really be over between Maxine and I. She has been on my mind heavily and I don't know what to do." "Have you tried to visit her or call?" "Of course I have, but she does not want to hear anything I have to say." "You must have done something serious." "I don't even want to talk about it." Allison nodded and walked back out of the office. She knew not to press the issue if I didn't volunteer any information. The next second Allison reappeared and handed me a receipt to sign. "What's this?" "For the flowers you sent Ms. Styles this morning." I just looked at her and signed the receipt. "Every little bit helps." Allison said as she left back out of my office. It seemed like only yesterday that we were making love and protesting our love for each other and today I'm begging. "Damn." I said out loud, "Things are really fucked up now." I busied myself with work that I had neglected to make the time pass. I was so deep in thought that I didn't hear a knock at my door. It wasn't until the figure reached my desk that I even noticed anyone there. "Into your work or ignoring me?" "What?" I looked up and Wendy was standing there. "Into your work or ignoring me, I said." "Wendy, I really don't feel like speaking with you. Please get out before you are out permanently." "Justice, I came to apologize. I didn't realize that you were into that chick so deep. A sista's gotta try you know. Anyway, it's been eating me up to see you off your comfort level around here and for me to know I'm the cause don't sit well believe it or not. I can't stand to be around you any longer knowing what I did, because no matter how I may come on to you, it's genuine. I really am attracted to you and it hurts to be rejected. So, I am resigning today. I appreciate you not firing me after what I pulled. But I think I have outstayed my welcome here." "I don't know what to say, thank you for being an adult about this. Maybe you should work on your approach to men Wendy. If you have to act the way you do to get someone interested in you, then that person is not for you." I stood up and walked over to her. "You are a very attractive woman, don't shortchange yourself." I shook her hand and she thanked me and began to walk out the door. "I hope you two have worked it out already." "Well, no. I think that relationship has ended." I turned around and faced the window trying to control my emotions. I only heard the door close and I slumped back down into my chair. Allison buzzed me and told me a phone call was on hold for me. "Justice Dane." I said as I answered the phone. "Mr. Dane, haven't spoken to you in a while, how's business?" "Mr. James, good to hear your voice. Everything's fine here, to what do I owe the pleasure?" "Well, we are having a few of our clients over this afternoon to pitch a new advertising angle. I wanted to see if you could make it. This should increase your sales 35% over what we are already promising." "Sounds great, I'll be there." Great. Now I have to sit in a room pretending to listen when all I am doing is staring at Maxine. Hopefully she won't be there and I can concentrate on business.

I arrived at Smith and Cohen and sat in my jeep and took a long deep breath. "I am going to go in here and conduct my business. Justice you are the man, what are sweating this female for? This isn't like you. Pull it together Sweet Nupe." I ran my hand on my hair and around my mustache. I needed to pump myself up before I made a fool of myself. I made my way to the elevator and to the receptionist desk. "Good evening Mr. Dane, right this way." I walked on with the secretary and past Maxine's office. I looked in as I passed and caught a glimpse of her. I could see her turning to look at me as I passed the glass enclosure of her office. I returned her glance and walked on. I noticed the roses that Allison sent her on her desk. At least she didn't throw them out. I wanted to turn back around and talk to her, but I had to stay professional. Bob greeted me at the door and offered me a seat. There were two other companies represented there and Bob sat down and buzzed his secretary. "Please ask Ms. Styles and Mr. Goldberg to join us. Gentlemen, we will be ready to begin as soon as our top Reps join us." Dammit. I thought I wasn't going to have to sit through this. Maxine and the other guy came in and introduced themselves around the room. Bob motioned for her to sit across from me in eye contact distance from each other. "Nice to see you again Mr. Dane." She said as she sat down. "The pleasure is mine Ms. Styles." I said trying to be cordial. Through the whole presentation, I could tell she was trying not to look in my direction. I tried to focus on the presentation, but I kept glancing at her. A few times, I caught her moving her eyes quickly back to the front of the room. Perhaps she felt me staring and glanced over to see if I was still looking. Or perhaps she wanted to look at me too. I felt like a high school kid stealing looks at a girl I had a crush on. I felt like writing her a letter saying will you go out with me yes or no. The presentation was finally over and everyone gathered to talk. I walked over to Bob and we talked about moving things toward what he suggested. I was anxious to leave before I was forced to grab her. I said my good-byes and walked towards the door. Maxine walked in front of me and shook my hand to make things seem like we were at least still doing business together. "See you next time Mr. Dane." She walked back into the office and turned again. "Thanks for the flowers." She whispered. I said nothing and walked on to the elevator. I was so excited that she even acknowledged me. Maybe I was going to stand a chance after all. I wanted to give her some more time so I left it at that.

Monique Lawton

You, Me, and He...

"Whew! That man knows how to look good." I said to myself walking back to my office. It was good seeing Justice today. Through all of this heartache, I still love him. I don't know if I can bring myself to forgive him, although every inch of me wants to throw myself at him and beg to be back together. I know he wants to make things right between us, but I just can't get those images of him and that ho out of my mind. "Oh well." I plopped down in my chair and tried to think about work and not Mr. Dane. I looked out my window watching the rain fall against it and then absorbed myself back into my work. It wasn't until I heard Cynthia over the intercom asking if I would see a Wendy that I even looked up from my desk. "Wendy? Who is Wendy?" I said as I pressed the intercom to give my reply. "Yes, send her in." I didn't know anyone named Wendy and I was not expecting anyone. My thoughts were interrupted by the knock on my door. "Come in." You could have knocked me over with a feather when I saw who walked through my door. That stinking, skanky ho that was straddled all over my man was walking through my office door. This bitch had a lot of nerve coming here. "I know what you are thinking, this bitch has a lot of nerve coming here." She said as she closed the door behind her. If she only knew how right she was. "Is there something I can help you with." I said with professionalism and a hint of attitude. "I know I am one of the last people you would want to see, but I had to see you and explain some things." "Did Justice put you up to this?" I said sitting down wanting to put my foot up her ass. "No. In fact I haven't seen him ever since I resigned. But he is the reason why I did come. He hasn't been the same around the office since you two broke up. I thought that everything would be fine between you, but I couldn't stand myself when I saw him dragging around and looking like his heart was torn from his chest." She sat down and put her coat over the chair. I don't know what she was getting comfortable for, surely she didn't think that she would be here that long. She continued, "I have always been after Mr. Dane. Can you blame any woman for being attracted to him? Mostly I thought that throwing myself at him would advance me in the Company. I was always doing things to try to get him in the bed, but he was never responsive. I knew you were seeing him, but I didn't take that into consideration. All I wanted to do was to get him to sleep with me so I could have a guaranteed elevator ride to the top. He never gave me a second thought when I would act slutty around him and he never spoke down to me for doing it. Even after I tore his world apart, he still told me that I was worth more than I give myself credit for. So this is why I had to come and correct things." She moved closer to my desk and looked me right in my eyes. "That day you came in was just another one of my efforts on him to try to break his will power. He was really trying not to over power me so he just kept his distance and kept telling me to put my clothes back on and get out. I knew he would not push me out so I kept on. He is such a gentle man and I have never seen him even raise his voice. I took advantage of that and made my way on top of him. He was really agitated at that point and told me to get off of him. I still insisted on trying to kiss him and he moved his face away and asked me to get off of him again. That is the exact moment you walked in. He didn't have a chance to force me off even though I think he was about to. He still didn't yell at me when you left, he just pulled me off and told me to leave. That made me feel so small and it made me realize how much he loved you and how faithful he is. Now you can take what I have told you and make amends with that man or you can be a damn fool and let him slip away. There are a lot of females that would do anything to be in your shoes. I know, I did." She got up and gathered her things. "Anyway, I'm sorry and I hope this clears things up for you. Good luck." She walked towards the door and left me as dumbstruck as she did when she walked in. I was in tears. All this time I doubted Justice and he has been suffering without me. And he didn't do anything with her. I immediately dialed his office and reached his secretary. She told me that he went home early and I slammed down the phone. I had to get to him to talk things over before it was too late. I felt so desperate, like it was already too late for us. I put on my coat and raced for the elevator. I rushed to my car and jumped in.

The rush hour traffic was even heavier because of the rain. "Why don't people in Atlanta know how to drive in the freaking rain." I yelled to the car in front of me. I was about to explode with excitement. I could finally give in and be with Justice again. I always felt that he was my soul mate, but after seeing him with Wendy made me think back to all those guys who dogged me. I thought because he was so perfect that he would be just like them. But maybe he was perfect because of the way I felt about him. "No, No, No!" I yelled out loud. My gaslight was blinking. "I don't have time to stop and get gas." I yelled at the light. "Go back out. I can make it." I made my way through the traffic and onto Old National Highway. I had to get to Justice. I made it half way to the entrance to his subdivision before my car conked out. I pulled it to the side of the road and slammed my fist against the steering wheel. I sat there for a moment and then grabbed my purse and hopped out of the car. The rain was falling harder but I didn't care, I had something to take care of. Cars kept whizzing by me splashing the rain in my direction soaking me from head to toe. I jogged all the way to the driveway that led to Justice's house. I knew I probably looked a mess, but I ran up to the door and rang the bell. I was freezing and shivering but my future waited for me on the other side of that door, so nothing else mattered. I saw the lights come on inside the glass block foyer and then the door opened. "Hi." I said, as Justice stood there with a happy and confused look on his face. He grabbed me and kissed me so passionately. We stood there for what seemed to be eternity holding each other. He finally moved back and looked at me. "I had to talk to you and my car ran out of gas down the street." He pulled me into the house and began to kiss me again. "I have missed you so much Maxine. I am so glad you came." He walked me over to the kitchen and we sat down. "Wendy came by my office and told me everything. I am so sorry I never listened to you. I should have known you better than that." "I'm sorry for even allowing her to get that close to me. I never meant to hurt you Maxine. All I ever wanted to do was love you and for you to love me." He held my hands and kissed them. "Can we put this behind us and start over?" "Are you kidding. I have been killing myself trying to figure a way to get you back. I am glad that you believed her and gave me another chance." He pulled me up from the chair. "Let's get you out of these wet clothes." We went upstairs and into his bedroom. I almost forgot how nice his place was. "I see you got a new statue in the hall, it's nice." "I needed a reminder of you. The artist sculpted it from a picture of you." "Oh baby." I kissed him on his cheek. He ran water in the Jacuzzi and lit candles around the edges. He always knew how to set the mood. "Just relax." He said as he pulled off the soaked blouse I had on. I sat on the bed and kicked my shoes off. Justice pulled my hose down sliding each foot from the wet nylon. I missed his touched. I almost exploded from just the thought of what he might be thinking of doing to me. This was definitely a sex moment. "May I?" He said looking for permission to pull my skirt off. "Yes." I said with a smile. He pulled off the rest of my clothes and I stood before him naked. "I must be dreaming." He said making me feel uneasy about being naked in front of him after all this time. I started to cover up and he moved my hands out the way. "I know this body, what are you covering up? Just because we have been apart doesn't mean I have forgot you. I have imagined you every way I can almost everyday." He ran his hands across my arms and kissed me. We moved to the tub and I got in. He left back out and turned on some music. The water felt so wonderful against my skin that I just sunk into it. "Mr. Entertainer." I thought to myself as I relaxed to the music and candlelit room and closed my eyes. Justice came back into the bathroom with a towel wrapped around his waist. Damn, that man knew how to keep his body in shape and looking too good. "Want some company?" He said waltzing over to the tub with a smooth stride. "I was getting lonely." I said eyeing his muscles. He dropped the towel and smiled. I think his dick had actually gotten a lot bigger since I saw it last. He was a fine man and I was anxious to see what the night had in store. He slid into the water easily. "Why do women bathe in such hot ass water?" I splashed him as he slid behind me. "I don't know if you know it or not, but you are mine girl." I smiled to myself and pulled his arms around me. I laid my head on his chest and it felt like my whole world was right again.

Reunion

"Fortunate to have you girl, I'm so glad you're in my world, just as sure as the sky is blue, I was blessed the day that I met you." I sung in her ear as she laid her head on my chest. I always got her going when I sang in her ear. She giggled and sunk deeper in my chest. Of all the things that Wendy messed up, she got this one right. I'll make sure she gets a good job offer for hooking me up. She did owe this to me for fucking things up, but still, I was extremely grateful. I cupped the water and ran it over Maxine's body. I picked up the brush from the edge of the tub and began to brush her hair. It was wet from the rain and I figured she needed the attention. Besides, I wanted to guarantee that I got some makeup booty! A man has needs, and it had been too long since I got some. Videotapes and jacking off had gotten old, so I had to be up on my best game. Even though it was genuine with her, it was still game. "That feels so good Justice." She said breaking my thoughts. "I know something else that feels better." I said kissing her neck. "You are so bad, three months and you haven't changed a bit." "Hey, I gotta keep it real." She hit me on my arm playfully and I grabbed her kissing her ears. "I missed this." She moaned as I rubbed her body. I loved to hear her moan like that, it turned me on. I turned her around and plunged my tongue in her mouth. She returned the kiss and our lips locked over each other. I pulled her closer to me and caressed her body. "I want you." I whispered in her ear as my lips ran over her ear. She moaned agreeably and wrapped her arms around my neck. I picked her up out of the tub and laid her on the fluffy wool rug that covered a portion of the marble floor. Her body glistened in the deep rug that surrounded her. I cuffed my mouth around her nipples and bit them gently. She rubbed my head as I ran my tongue along her breasts and stomach. I pulled back to her mouth and kissed her with all the love I had inside of me. She reached down and rubbed my balls as I continued to kiss her. Spreading her legs apart, I looked at her, "I love you." With tears in her eyes, she managed to choke out the words; "I love you Justice." I guided myself inside her and she let out a wonderful moan that made me tremble. With every stroke I kissed her even harder and she grabbed me tighter. "Maxine." I heard myself say as I took longer deeper strokes. I never called out anybody's name before; this had to be the one for me. She pulled me closer to her body and moan with excitement. "You feel so good, you feel so good." She panted out as I slowed down my strokes to a slow grind. I pulled out and picked her up to lay her butt on the sink. The mirrors caught every angle of our bodies as she gave me that wild tiger look in her eyes that turned me on so. I entered her again and she rested her back against the mirror. The sight of her body moving with my strokes excited me and I plunged faster. "Faster baby." She groaned and I sped up my strokes. She gasped and pulled her body close to mine. We both exploded and held each other. I was breathing heavily and she was getting heavy, so I carried her to the bed. We were both dry by now and after wiping each other off, we slipped into the covers. "Is it always going to be like this?" She asked. "If I keep in shape, I guess I can swing it." "That's not what I meant silly." She said laughing. "Is it always going to be so wonderful being with you, making love like love and not just fucking? Feeling like the world doesn't matter because I'm with you?" I pulled her to my face, "I guarantee it."

A New Day

We awoke together with smiles on our faces. I felt like I was living in a Jill Scott song. "Now that we're back together I wanted to know where we are going from here." He said as we lay in the bed snuggling. "Well, I really haven't been thinking about that lately Justice." "That's all I've been thinking about. I want to take this to another level. I am not about to let you slip away again." He turned to face me. "I want you to move in with me. Now I know what happened to you before, but this is different. I plan on taking it further than just shacking. I'm not asking for an answer now, just think about it." "I'll think about it Justice. I want to move on to new grounds with you as well. I'm trying my best to not rely on my past as a reference to all of this. Give me a few days to think it over." He kissed me on my face. "That's all I ask, no pressure. Get dressed so we can go get your car before it gets towed." I forgot all about the car. We both got dressed and left the house. He put gas in my car and I went home to freshen up. When I got home there were two messages on my machine. I pressed the button to retrieve them. "Where are you? I called the office and your cell. Please give me a call, I'm worried." It was Simone. I forgot to call her and give her the news. The next message came through, "Hello Maxine, this is Bryce, the guy you met at the club. I know it's been a couple of weeks, but I just found your number, long story that involves my ex

117

cleaners. Hope I'm not too late. My number is (404) 555-9750, give me a call I want to see you." I forgot all about that guy. I sure did not want to get into anything with him. I am still ashamed of the way I acted with him, and letting him kiss and feel over me was messed up. "Oh well." I erased his message and I dialed Simone. "Where you been?" She yelled in the phone. "Well hello to you too. If you must know I was in Fayetteville." "What, with Justice? What happened?" She said all at once. "That ho I caught him with came to my office yesterday." "What? You kick her ass?" "I know right? She was cool. She told me that she was the one who forced that situation and Justice never touched her. I left my office and headed straight for his house and now he wants me to move in with him." "Damn, I missed everything. Are you going to move in with him?" She said taking in the news. "I don't know. I'm trying to weigh my options without thinking about that jackass Fabian." "Please don't. This is a whole 'nother level here. You can't even compare the two." "I know. Guess who called me last night? That cute guy I met at the club." "After all this time? Wow how interested was he?" She said sarcastically. "He said something happened with his cleaners." "Well he's too late. And you better hope how you acted with him don't get out. I was on my way out the door. I'm going over to Shawn's." "What ya'll doing?" "Making plans. I'll tell you about it later." "See, you holding back too." "Ha, and I'm going to leave you hanging too. Bye." Simone hung up the phone. Her and Shawn must be having the same talk I just had with Justice. It's about time for them, they have been putting this off for far too long now. I decided to turn on some music and clean up. My apartment was in a wreck and I had some free time on my hands. I was just about finished when the phone rang. "Hey baby what you doing?" It was Justice. "Nothing, just cleaning up." "I just got off the phone with Shawn. Him and Simone want to meet us at the club. They have some news they want to tell us and hang out a little." "I bet they are finally about to get married or something." I said with excitement. "Yeah, it's something like that. Anyway, get dressed, I'll pick you up about 10:00." "Okay baby, I'll be ready." I couldn't wait. The suspense was killing me. My girl was finally settling down. I had a big kool-aid smile on my face, but it left when I started thinking about myself. Now the pressure was going to be on me to give Justice an answer. I don't know if I want to make that step just yet. And I damn sure don't want him to get away. I looked at the clock, it was already 9:00. "Shit, I better get my butt in gear." I said as I went to my closet to see what I was going to wear. I threw one of my sexy outfits on the bed and fixed my hair. It was frizzy from the rain last night. It was a little after ten when I heard my doorbell.

"Hey baby." I said grabbing her around her waist. "Shawn better be glad he my boy, cause as good as you look I want to stay in." "You better watch out, I just might take you up on that." She kissed me and pulled away. "Let me get my shoes and I'll be ready." We pulled up in the parking lot of the club and saw Shawn and Simone. We went into the club and got a seat in VIP. "So what's up, we are dying to know." I said as soon as we sat down. Maxine nudged me. "Let them tell us themselves." "What? Don't act like you don't want to know." Simone and Shawn just laughed. "Well, that's what we asked you to come down here for. Tonight we celebrate. I asked Simone to marry me and she said yes." "I knew it." Maxine screamed and gave Simone a hug. She showed us her ring. He gave her a big rock. "Congratulations man. I'm proud of you." I slapped Shawn five and gave him a hug. "This occasion deserves champagne. I'll be right back." I went to the bar to get some Moet. Maxine and Simone got up and went to the restroom. Women always want to go to the restroom and freshen up. That's just another way of saying they have to gossip in private. I went to the bar and ordered two bottles of Moet for our table. I was about to go back to the table when I heard somebody call me from behind. "Justice, what's up?" "Oh what's up Phi?" It was my sands from Hampton, Bryce. He was an image consultant. He designed clothes and cut hair in a storefront loft. He had a good business and he did magic on people, even I used him to tighten a brotha up. "You hanging out with the middle class?" He gave me a hug. "You know me, keeping it real. Shawn just got engaged man, we are celebrating with our girls." "What? Shawn? The world must be about to end." We both laughed.

"Oh shit." Bryce said looking behind me. "You see that tease right there?" I turned around and saw that he was pointing to Maxine. "I met her a couple of weeks ago. Homegirl danced with me grinding all over me and shit. She had a brother dick hard as steel. I watched her at the bar guzzling down a few drinks and I knew she was feeling right so I asked her to dance. She dances like one of those tricks down at Nikki's. I almost got some too, but she wasn't that drunk. I tongued her down and we were going to get busy in the hall. I have to get a taste of that. I called her yesterday, but she never called me back. I would go over and holler at her but I'm with my girl. I gotta find out if she fucks the way she dances. Anyway, stay up man, call me." I couldn't say anything. How was I supposed to tell my boy that was my lady? What the fuck was she doing showing her ass like that in public. That was one of the things that attracted me to her, she was classy. Can't any old hoodrat be seen with me and that is what she acted like. And my boy caught her out of pocket like that. My whole night was fucked up after that shit. I went back to the table and waited for our waiter. "You sure are quiet all of a sudden." She said kissing my neck. I turned away playing it off that I was rejecting her. She kind of looked at me and then turned to talk to Simone. "So Justice, I hear that you have been thinking about some changes in your relationship." Simone said with Maxine hitting her on the leg. "Well looks like the champagne is here." I said as the waiter walked up to the table with glasses. "Let me propose a toast, to two people who love each other the way love is supposed to be. Congratulations." "How poetic." Shawn said. The rest of the night all I could think about was that bullshit with Maxine. She kept asking me what was wrong, but I told her nothing. I tried to be social so I wouldn't ruin the evening for Shawn and Simone. I was glad when everybody was ready to go. We got in the car and I didn't have anything to say.

Here We Go Again

"Why are you going this way, I thought I was spending the night at your place?" I said as I noticed he was turning onto 75 north. "You're taking me home?" I asked him. "I thought you wanted to go home." "What's with you? You asked me to stay with you this weekend." "Fine, we'll go to my place, damn." He turned the car around quickly and sped on the southbound lane. I didn't know what happened, but ever since he came from the bar he was acting strange. I thought that maybe he was tired so I didn't say anything else the whole ride to his house. When we pulled into his driveway, he got out and slammed the car door. He usually would wait for me to get out the car and then open the door to the house for me, but he walked up to the door and just went inside. I came into the house and he walked upstairs. I closed the door behind me puzzled at this point. I walked up the stairs and went into the bedroom. He plopped on the bed and put a pillow over his face. "Who are you and what have you done with Justice?" I said pulling the pillow from his face. He snatched it back down and said nothing. "Did I miss something? One minute you ask me to move in with you, the next I'm public enemy number one." "You are a public something, ho maybe." He mumbled from under the pillow. "Excuse me. What did you just say?" I snatched the pillow from his face. His eyes were blood shot red and tears were streaming down his face. He looked so angry. "What in the hell is wrong with you?" He jumped up from the bed and got in my face. "What's wrong with you?" He walked away to calm himself down. I was totally confused now. He began to speak with his back turned to me. "I'm out with my lady having a good time. Then I run into my boy Bryce and he starts telling me about some tease who freaked him on the dance floor and got his dick hard and he wondered if she fucked the way she danced. Then when I turn around, he's talking about you." My mouth dropped to the floor. I could not believe that that night came back to haunt me. It's a small world, you never know who knows who anymore. He had every right to be upset so I decided to explain. "I went out with Simone that night you came over. I was upset and had a few drinks." He interrupted me. "Oh I know. You were acting like a fucking alcoholic. Is this how you act every time you get upset? Is this the image I have to look forward to? Everybody thinking I have a fucking lush ass freak for a girlfriend?" I have never seen him like this. The ghetto really came out in him. His words hit me hard and I felt them all the way in my soul. "Is that all you think about is your image? I was upset and I didn't think rationally. All I did was dance with him and we were not together at that point." He walked back in my face. "All you did was dance? If I wanted a ho I would have fucked Wendy." I slapped him. How dare he put me in the same category as that skank? He walked into the bathroom and slammed the door. I picked up the phone and called a cab. I was not staying there to fuel things up any farther. He needed some time to calm down and think about what he said. This was the exact reason why I did not want to move in with him. You never know who that person your sleeping with will turn into. It took about thirty minutes and the cab beeped. I walked out without saying anything. Things had turned back around for us. This time it was me who had messed things up and it hurt. I saw Justice looking out the window as I pulled off. I guess he had time to calm down, but it was too late. The damage had already been done.

I called Shawn to ask his opinion on this one. I wanted to go after her and talk about what happened, but my pride was holding me back. He picked up after a few rings. "What's wrong?" He said sounding like I interrupted something. "I'm sorry man, I need to talk to you." "What's up?" "I just had a fight with Maxine. I blew up on her." "You were acting strange all night, what happened?" I took a deep breath at the thought of explaining this one. "I saw Bryce at the bar and he told me that he met Maxine a couple of weeks ago and she danced with him all nasty like a stripper. You know how it is coming from somebody you know. And he said he kissed her and almost got with her." "Damn. I didn't know she was like that." "Exactly. She said she had a few drinks and she was upset with me." "That's how women do. They get all upset and wind up doing something they regret. He didn't hit it did he?" "Naw, but he called her to set it up." "Did she talk to him?"

"No." "Then what you beefing for? You love this woman right?" "Yes, but..." "But nothing. You love her you forgive her. She forgave you. And you said it yourself, she didn't even do anything with him. What's a dance? You just got back in and now you mad at each other again? Ya'll ever going to be right?" He made a lot of sense. "She just caught a cab and went home. I said some things that I shouldn't have." "You need to go over there and get things straight. Don't let that petty mess stand between your happiness. That woman is going to be your wife, you know that." Shawn was right, but I think I messed up with her again mentioning Wendy. "I'll get up with you later, thanks man." I hung up with him and got in my car. I never saw her cry, so maybe I had a good chance of getting back in. We needed to talk about our expectations of each other. I did not want to go down this road again. I know she was confused because of the way I blew up. I had to assure her that it would never happen again. I pulled into the parking lot of her apartment. I could see her in the window walking back and forth. I caught the front door with another couple going into the building. As the elevator reached her floor I started to feel anxious. "Here we go again." I mumbled to myself and knocked on the door. "Who is it?" She asked from behind the door. "Baby, it's me. Open the door." "Go away Justice. I don't want to fight with you." "If you don't open the door, I'm going to get loud out here." She always had a thing about you getting loud with her in public. It embarrassed the hell out of her. The door opened and she walked away. She walked to her couch and sat down facing the window. "I came to apologize. I had no right getting so upset and talking to you like that. And I know the fact that I even mentioned Wendy pissed you off even more. I was wrong. Can you look at me please, I don't like talking to your back." I pulled her around to face me. "It's just that I see you as my queen. To me you are a virgin and it just tore my heart to know that my boy saw you in another way. When I first saw you, you walked into that restaurant with your head high looking like a million bucks. You were so classy. I noticed you as soon as you walked in. Your shit was tight and I wanted to know you. I was about to put my sweetest mack moves on you until I found out you were my business date. All I thought about was you from that point on. And every time I saw you, it was the same. You are a beautiful woman and you got it going on. I felt so much joy and pride when you became mine. And it's not just your looks, don't get me wrong. I don't need a trophy. You are beautiful on the inside too. And we fit together so well. So you see, this is what upset me so much. My boy only saw you as a piece of ass because of the way you carried on that night. He didn't see what I saw in you. It angers me to see women do that to themselves and it angered me even more because it was the woman I loved doing it to herself." Tears began to run down her face. "I love you Maxine. I love you with all my heart and soul. I make this promise to you that you will never see me act that way again. Never." She began to choke out an apology. "I'm so sorry Justice. I should have not tried to get revenge like that. I let the alcohol control me and I know I can't handle liquor well, especially when I am upset like I was. I will never drink like that anymore." I pulled her closer to me and held her tight. "The answer to your question is yes." I backed up and looked at her. "What question?" "Will I move in with you? My answer is yes." I looked at her and smiled. I was so happy. "Baby, we are going to make this work. You will not be sorry. We are going to be like George and Weezy!" I hugged her tight again and kissed her passionately. "I just can't get you out my system. It's like that old song, I got the sweetest hangover I don't want to get over." "It's called love and that's what we got. You can't get over it." "I never want to." She said and kissed me. Everything was the way it was supposed to be and I hoped nothing was going to change. I had the woman of my dreams in my arms again and this time I was going to do whatever it took to keep her there.

About the Author

Monique Lawton was born in the Bronx, New York and raised in the suburbs of Atlanta, Georgia where she currently resides with her husband and two sons. She is an active member of her community, serving through her membership in Delta Sigma Theta Sorority, Incorporated. Her career path has taken her from obtaining a Bachelor's degree in Architecture, to managing several Banking centers. She now expands her attributes to following a passion for writing. Look for more exciting novels to come from this young writer.